FROM STORMY SEAS TO CALMER WATERS

A STORY OF AUTISM, LOSS AND SPIRITUAL GROWTH

Áine Crosse
With chapter contributions from Gerry Crosse

DEDICATION

This book is dedicated to our family and to both those who face so many daily challenges dealing with children with additional needs and to their loved ones who relentlessly support them. May they grow and thrive.

Most importantly, the book is dedicated to my husband, Gerry, who tragically passed in June 2020. He was our rock and was entirely dedicated to his children. We will love and miss him forever.

Back Row: Dean, Adam, Gerry, Áine and Ryan
Front Row: Darragh, Sean, Lisa, and Amy

ACKNOWLEDGEMENTS

—•—

We would like to thank our Publishing House and, in particular, our excellent Editors John O' Donnell and Susan McKenna. Gratitude to Sharon Blaney for being an unfailing source of support and positivity in our lives, and the aforementioned John for his patience and support during the writing of this book. We would also like to thank Niall MacGiolla Bhuí, from The Book Hub Publishing Group for his continuing support and for bringing this book to life. It's one of the upsides of having written this book that we now count Susan and Niall as friends. Finally, we would like to say a huge thank you to Dean, Ryan, Amy and Adam for being such wonderful siblings to Darragh, Seán and Lisa. Their loving support is truly unconditional and we, as parents, are forever grateful.

TABLE OF CONTENTS

INTRODUCTION
WHY US?

——•◦•——

At times, we wonder how it all happened, how we got to this point in our lives. We began to think about why this had happened to us, what we had done to deserve this. It took us years to realise that nothing we had done had caused this; it was simply a result of things beyond our control.

It could be so easy to label ourselves as victims. To be honest, we felt life had let us down. We have very sick children with a disease that cannot be cured. We learned that they also have autism and then another blow; I was also given a serious diagnosis. Any person with all of this weight to carry might well feel like a victim, so why shouldn't we? Why shouldn't we both say "why me?" We're sure many parents of children with autism reading this book may well feel the same. It's ok to say this. In fact, we believe it's crucial that you do. Saying it out loud both allows you to admit it and then deal with it. We were victims, if we even use that word, of a difficult and deeply complex set of circumstances. We have discovered, however, that there is more to this; it doesn't end here, not like this, not for us. This admission helped us to feel empowered, and to believe that we could, somehow, find a way through the highs and lows in this story called "life." But. More challenges were to come the way of our family unit. More of this later.

PART I
THE BEGINNING

CHAPTER ONE
INTO THE
UNKNOWN

—•—

They say that the biggest sacrifice that a person can give is to lay down their life for someone they love. And in that, we talk about sacrifice in terms of death; an end. What very few people tell you is that a life can be laid down without ever dying at all. This becomes a living state not like what any of us ever imagine. In our own future, all our great sacrifices are made with time — great big chunks of it offered up for the sake of progress. And in this dream of the future, you see the best version of you — happy, alive, and full of ambition. There is a blueprint carved out by your hand. And what follows in the end is the lesson that these great plans of ours are made and broken on the rock, and the only true constant is how hard we fight against all the things that life throws in our path.

In my own future, I imagined versions of myself. I was a socialite who dreamed of going to college and studying makeup. I wanted to be a beautician, to go into a world of models and fashion. What I wanted was completely opposite to being a parent. I liked the glamorous side of life, and I liked the idea of living it without limitations. I didn't want kids. These were my plans. I recognize that most people find contentedness around the 9 - 5, the basic blueprint; you're born, you go to school, you get a job, you get married, you have children, you work for forty years until you retire and at the end of it all, you enjoy your twilight years in peace as you watch your grandchildren grow and flourish. I'd always admired that great sacrifice - laying down your life for someone you love - the great act of childbirth.

Imagine, then, waking up one morning, and despite having done everything right, despite having taken all the steps specified in your blueprint to stay on that track to find that beautiful thing you imagined gone from you and the shape of it now barely visible on the horizon. This was how I found out, at the age of 20, that I was becoming a mother.

Dean was born on December 6th, 1992 and all of it was strange and surreal. What was I to do with this little person? I loved children from a distance, the children of other mothers and their laughter and their quirks —but here now was my own and I had no idea how I could even begin to accept this great ripple in the middle of my grand design. Truth be known, I didn't even know how I'd come to be pregnant with Dean. I was naive when it came to many things. I was just a child having a child. And yet, though no one advised me, I fell into the role as if it was always meant to be.

Then, in May of '96, I gave birth to my second chuld — Ryan. He was a bundle of kindness who grew up with a somewhat reserved personality, and a whole wheelbarrow of warmth and intelligence. He became such a source of unexpected wisdom and advice as he grew older, when it became more important than ever. By now, with Ryan's birth, motherhood was an unavoidable fact peppered with the occasional moment of disbelief as I stood there in the kitchen cutting crusts from sandwiches and packing lunches I had never signed up to pack. You're sitting there watching all your friends doing their thing and you can't live the life you want because suddenly you're expecting a new baby. In the end, I never even finished school. Nonetheless, the pattern continued and I was beside myself and besotted with the birth of Amy two years later. More and more, I was beginning to think that blueprints and grand plans were a plaything of the universe and I was just a vehicle to carry out this new storyline. Still, in spite of that version of myself from six years ago, here was the girl that I had hoped for after six years of boys and men. She was everything I could ever want— and certainly I hoped in spite of what everyone thinks. I wanted to braid her hair and surround her with dolls and lose myself in this new experience of having a girl, at last.

I had three wonderful children, and I loved them. Each one of them. And all of a sudden, my first marriage came to an abrupt and irreversible end.

Left with three children and a broken marriage, the world becomes a different place — it was just early nights, and even earlier mornings; it was at odds with everything that I was at 20. That version of me now lay somewhere far, far from here and now. When I left my previous husband and I was on my own, alone in the house; I couldn't sleep. I lost a part of myself —and I did lose a part of myself. There had been someone there that was a part of everything—and suddenly there wasn't; I used to sit at night looking out the window, never sleeping and living out of fear. And somewhere along the way, in the middle of all that loneliness—I found Gerry.

Without ever believing it possible, Gerry became my knight in shining armour, taking us all on and allowing something new that made our family feel whole again. A fresh start. And like anyone, we came to imagine our happy ever after as one filled with children of our own alongside my wonderful boys and my wonderful Amy. I believed then that I would come to have the family I now wanted more than my long—gone self could ever have imagined, and with a man I felt as though I knew all my life, even though I just met him. But that was not how it was to be.

Adam

In the year of '02, I gave birth to Adam. Adam was my first born child with Gerry, and four years later we were pregnant with Darragh. The house we lived in became too small for our growing family and we decided that it was time to put ourselves into a bigger house. We started looking for a new home, one that we could actually buy and call our own. Life had taken on a new shape — One that felt natural; one that felt right and hopeful; one that promised good things, and things were at last changing for the better and we were, with neither doubt nor fear, feeling excited for our new future with our children.

As a child, Adam appeared to develop as any child would —with the exception of needing assistance with his speech and language. At that time, we weren't overly worried to discover this as Dean, our eldest, also needed assistance in his earlier years. He gurgled and laughed at all the things that children do, and along with Darragh who came later, they carved up the floors chasing one another, eating like there was no tomorrow. We had the same worries that every other parent had; and the same joys; and the same boring routines; and the same dreams for our children that you might expect.

This is what being a parent is supposed to look like, the kind of parenting that you see in media and television, the sort of thing that everyone normally expects when they're thrown into the whole affair, and the sort of thing that every non-parent imagines when they put together their own version of it in their heads. And if there was any indication of the difficulties that were about to unfold about us, or how often we would begin to wake up not knowing how to cope, or how every single thing was about to become frightening and hopeless and impossible, then we saw none of it. We were about to step into a world of medical terms and complete unknowns; we needed a lot of courage, a determination and an unwavering faith in ourselves and in the medical world which we were about to become well acquainted with. I never saw it then as the biggest sacrifice I would eventually have to make. I didn't know. The way I see it is that kids grow up and do their thing and that was always their image; I never envisaged a future of having kids that would never leave me - or two of them at least. Parenthood, as we knew it, was about to be changed forever and completely. And that story begins with Darragh.

CHAPTER TWO
DARRAGH

—◦•◦—

I t takes a great deal of courage to face our worst fears when they show up and threaten everything we know. It feels like the end of the world. Not the end of the actual world which we often shove under the carpet and put off until tomorrow. When someone tells you that the world is ending through climate change or whatever else, people roll their eyes, they laugh a little and then they get on with their day. If you want to know fear, try remembering if you've paid the bills this month, or if the car insurance is due, or if the cupboards have been filled for the week. That's when your early morning goes from calm to panic. The difference between all of that is that no one expects the actual end of *your* world as you know it. You somehow always find the energy and the time to deal with the most typical problems, the ones that hold your attention; the ones that make people push big, worldly problems under the carpet until tomorrow. And somewhere in the middle of life, as I was dealing with all these smaller, boring parts of parenthood and expecting a new child, my world as I knew it turned into chaos and struggle and not knowing; matters of life and death. My world, as I knew it, really did begin to end. Nor did I realize that it was entirely too late to turn back. On this particular morning, my thoughts were half stuck in sleep and the other half verging on apprehension. There were only so many mornings left in this house in which we would soon no longer fit. Not now when we were expecting a new addition to the family. Darragh was born on the 10th of May, 2006. It was a typical mess but with a great deal more drama. They all said it was too soon, and I tried my best to convince them that the labour pains, the intense inhaling and exhaling, and the pain — was real.

"She's dilated, she IS in labour," a student nurse had said. No one believed her.

I was moved to a bath and given painkillers. Not once did anyone but that incredible student nurse imagine that ten minutes later, at the end of all that, that Darragh would be born in the annex ward. And we loved every part of him. As any mother will tell you, people have a very incomplete picture of the stresses of raising a newborn child. The sleeplessness and the crying, the demands made on your body and the stress this little bundle is capable of inflicting, and all of this is second to the worry that every mother has - is my child healthy? In the beginning, he cried and cried, and none of us knew why he was crying. His distress played with our sanity. He seemed to cry and you could never understand why. He was so different — as if he was sick from day one. A mother's instinct is like listening to an invisible train as you're standing on the tracks. Something was 'off' and nothing could shake the feeling that something was about to hit us. We became worried as we looked at our child and agreed that something was definitely wrong. Maybe it's some sort of gift granted at the door to parenthood - that feeling you get as a mother or father when you know that something is not right with your child. Whatever pressed us, it finally led us both to the same conclusion, that even though there was nothing obviously wrong - our child had to see a doctor. Until such a time, it would keep eating at us, this quiet feeling that grew stronger every time we looked from one child to another and saw in Darragh something that couldn't be explained away with logic. It never occurred to us that there would be questions, or how we would explain our thoughts. "What exactly is the problem?" a doctor asked, tapping his head as he looked from Darragh to us, sincerely.

I felt there was something not quite right with him, and I said as much. "His skin seems yellow, and something just doesn't seem right," I admitted. I have always felt very protected in life. I've also felt as though some unseen thing has always been there on the edge, guiding me when there was something wrong - with myself, with Gerry, with our children. This was what I felt. This same presence told me to take action, to talk to a doctor, to get over the doubt and to go with my gut. I've come to trust that instinct, and so that's what I did. But how could I tell that to the doctor? I wasn't going to admit that my worries were coming from something nobody could see, or he would have thought I was mad.

After a long chat with our doctor; back and forth for ages and ages, talking about what was to be done next with Darragh, he suggested that taking a urine sample was a good place to start. It didn't take very long to know my instincts were right, and for us to find out that Darragh had a kidney infection. Our immediate thought was something close to relief. I mean, a kidney infection - that happens to a lot of children, right? And that's how it started. Though, without knowing, we'd stepped onto this path some ten months ago, it was now that the first signs made themselves known that we were no longer in familiar territory, and that all of this was something else entirely. This was to be the start of a journey for all of us, one that would lead us down a road filled with test after test and oh, so many hospital visits.

Darragh was sent to hospital where they treated him for a kidney infection. We wanted to relax - after all, a kidney infection could be easily treated, and logic therefore dictated that our baby would be fine. When, then, did we feel something else creeping up on us? The worry just didn't go away. Neither Gerry nor I could understand why Darragh needed to go to hospital for a kidney infection. None of this felt right to us. We couldn't shake the feeling that there was something else, that something else was wrong with our baby. It started with a lot of things we didn't understand. I couldn't help but notice that Darragh seemed tense - at least, that's how it seemed to my rational brain. Six weeks into this journey of unknowns, I brought it to their attention. Darragh, as it turns out, was doing what they called "fisting" which is another term for not opening your hands and constantly having them in a fist. They took this as a sign - and signs were suddenly all we had. They told us little else.

It was decided that Darragh needed to see a Neurologist. This, I can now say, is something that life does not prepare you for. We were sent home after a few days, and then they asked us to return a week later to run more tests.

And more tests.

It was suggested, kindly, that we should christen him before coming back in for tests. As a mother, I couldn't help but take this as a red flag.

What was the rush? What was wrong with our baby? What was it that we were not being told? Every thought became a question. And in the absence of being able to do anything else, and armed with nothing but questions, we did as suggested and christened our child. It was a day filled with difficult emotions, with thoughts and fears and questions piling up in the corners. Despite our greatest efforts, I remember the overwhelming worry that ruined what should have been a happy celebration.

CHAPTER THREE
I'M NOT OK

There are ways in which being a mother overcomes every other part of you. You just suck it up and you get on with it. After the ceremony, it was this feeling, though I couldn't give it a name at the time, that went through me. In the middle of such a stressful time, the day demanded my attention when all I wanted was a corner of the world to find a little silence and a moment to breathe. Both Gerry and I had our families over for a party, but the entire time, I was terrified inside and sick with worry.

After the church, I tried to socialise downstairs with our guests. I tried to compose myself in some way and find the will, but it just wouldn't come. There are two sides to that day, two perspectives, two sets of memories — that part of me that played host to normality — or tried to — and the conflicted side that threatened to cannibalize the other which eventually succeeded. And so when I think back to that time, I remember both sets of memories; the conversations and the congratulations. My emotional stability looked like a motorway car crash. Everyone seemed to know what I tried to hide, that I wasn't right. I did a lot of walking, holding Darragh as though he might disappear from me at any moment.

Before long, I just couldn't hold my tears, and with Darragh in my arms, I went up to my room, I lay on my bed with this little bundle in my arms, and I cried for both of us. Deep down, I knew that the hospital was looking for something serious and that it was all completely out of my control. I felt like I was about to lose my baby boy, that I couldn't do anything to stop it, and as a parent that sense of helplessness — watching your child quietly lumber their way into calamity — that has to be the greatest fear imaginable. I sat in my bedroom with snowballing anxiety, thinking about the guests downstairs, how they were having a good time, and here I was upstairs — dying inside and terrified for my son; beside myself with fear for everything that might be wrong with him.

Gerry was my only connection to what seemed like a different planet downstairs. He asked me to come down, and I knew that nothing could push me to go back. He shouldered the responsibility so that I could breathe and I wanted to thank him in words. Whatever was in my mind must have shown itself in my face, and when he saw it — he understood. I just couldn't. I couldn't pretend that I was fine anymore, because the truth was that l wasn't. I was not ok.

It had all become too much. It was a time in my life that I imagined myself getting through by the skin of my teeth and condemning to a place it could never return from. I wouldn't have wished it on anyone. Nothing justified such a sense of loss without having lost anything at all. I should have spoken to those closest to me, but l felt that the moment l spoke out, the moment I let it out of my mind, that it would take shape, that I was making things real, that I was giving weight to my fears; things that hadn't even happened yet.

Talking, I've found in looking back, is much more useful than we ever give it credit for. How can you expect to fix a problem with one hand tied behind your back? Talking through our fears, with family or friends, brings you out of your own mind. It puts your fears before the world and renders them vulnerable to all the good, all the powerful thoughts that people are capable of, and fear is terrified of perspective. It lives on doubt. And that was all I had in that moment — fear and doubt. If I could go back to that day and say all the things that were going through my mind. If I could have put into words what was eating me from the inside to those who loved me, then I might not have felt so alone in a situation that, unbeknownst to me, I was never alone in to begin with.

And that is the power of doubt.

I returned to the hospital the morning after the christening and the tests began. Darragh had an MRI; an experience that is daunting to even the best of us adults. They followed up with a lumbar puncture (more commonly known as a spinal tap) — a procedure that involves sticking a terrifyingly large needle into your spinal canal to collect fluid under local anesthesia.

Darragh was three months old.

Blood tests followed which meant that my son had to suffer further punctures. I remember being so devastated while looking at my tiny baby having these horrible tests done. Can you, an adult, imagine the experience of having your spine coated in gel and then stuck with a needle? And then be told that this was just the beginning? That same feeling of helplessness painted that entire episode. I watched them performed on my baby, and it felt like my nightmares had somehow become real. I wanted to step in, to take all the pain. And yet here was this child, barely 12 weeks into the world and yet so helpless in his suffering.

I stayed with Darragh when he was in hospital. I slept on the floor on a mattress. I was tired. Hungry. Afraid.

And yet none of this needed to be. I put myself in this situation. I pushed people away, I felt I alone had to do this thing. After all, he is my child. Even the thought of leaving Darragh's side terrified me in case he woke up, and so I stayed — rarely moving, barely eating.

Both Gerry and my mother were in constant contact, ringing five times a day, asking questions as my brain struggled under stress to answer them. I had gotten myself into such a place that I felt there was no return. I imagined all the things that could be wrong with our son - a whole wave of problems. It's amazing how, with such a thing as your child being sick, that you can fall into such a negative place - one where you feel lost, where you've lost control of the outcome, and you suddenly find that you're unable to help your child.

I stopped taking calls. I just wanted to cry and be alone with my thoughts; thoughts that were not serving me, nor did they serve Darragh. None of it helped. To me, living was now not that much different from a nightmare. I spent each and every day in a hospital, watching what was happening with my child playing out like a story outside of my control. Finally, Gerry rang until the phone was more alive than my own wellbeing - over and over until I found the strength to answer it. "Talk to me, Áine. Your Mam - me - we're worried about you. Please." They were both concerned that, as I had suffered with postnatal depression after having Dean, that it might be happening again.

Watching this happening with our baby son, and feeling like it's my fault - because I gave birth to him... Darragh didn't ask for any of this.

In hindsight, it's my belief that this was Darragh's contract with the world. This was the price of living. And in this contract, Gerry and I had been chosen to walk with him, and that was our price for loving. I believe that we all have an invisible blueprint to our journey, given to us by the universe, and this was ours. This was our faith being tested. Ours and Darragh's.

CHAPTER FOUR
THE ROLE OF FAITH

————

A nd speaking of faith.

All of us have our own relationship, our own contract with the world. Some of us believe that we're alone in it, and others believe in something other than the self. I'm not here to tell you which one is better - only that without faith, I was going to be swallowed up. It kept me grounded. I've never really understood why faith is something everyone finds so hard to have. We know that there are consequences to our actions, good or bad, but we still commit to our actions just to see how far we can go. We ask for luck and well wishes, we pray for good things and pay attention to superstition, and when things go wrong, we then lose that same faith; in ourselves, in our choices, in God, in everything. We blame other people or other things, and still we return to luck and prayer and superstition time and time again.

Faith, however, is seeing the bigger picture — knowing that things are as they should be; knowing that if you are willing to believe in something bigger than yourself, you can accept that there are things beyond your control, that there will always be things you won't understand; choices and events and misfortune. Believing that this process is above you, working at all times under different names; be it fate, destiny, or whatever else. This belief gives you the freedom to make peace with what you can't change, and to change what you can in order to move forward.

I do not in any way wish to push my beliefs on anyone but I do know that from time to time, we all look up and see that the world is so much bigger than us, and that we are only a part of it. There is so much more than we understand, and there is so much that is connected that we can't see. We all touch upon people in different ways whether we realise it or not. Each person leaves an impression and shapes us, playing some purpose be it big or small. Everyone plays a part. And when we start to see this, we begin to see how complex life can be, maybe a blueprint of a kind, a plan and a purpose for us here on this earth.

At the time l felt so alone in it all, without purpose, and without much of anything. Gerry worked long hours as an industrial fencer. Despite what worked demanded of him, he stayed in contact throughout the entire day - he, too, was a rock. It gave me something to stand on, and it made a huge difference. And still, I physically occupied this house on my own throughout the day; children dangling from each limb. We both knew that we needed the money. I knew that this was the way we had to do things. Throughout all of this, I had a lot of support from people around me, especially from my family. But faith was what kept me in a good place.

It is my faith that there is something bigger than us at work here. I believe in the mantra that it all happens for a reason. This was to be our journey, and though l didn't completely understand why, or even how we'd get through it, I wanted so desperately to have faith. Even as I began to push everyone away, even when Gerry came home in the evenings when I was too tired to talk;

physically, mentally, and emotionally. This tested our relationship in ways I can't describe, but when I look back, I realise how strong it made us, and how much we grew. That kind of pressure changes you. It changes your shape and you become something deeper. Where many other relationships would have cracked under less stress than what was now our 'normal', we somehow found a way to keep it all together. We loved each other, and we loved our family so much that we knew we had to keep it together. This wasn't just for us, it was for Darragh, too. I found the faith to believe that this was just a test; one made for us, and we made it because we had each other. No one could slow down or stop the difficulties, but sticking together and opening up the lines of communication - that kept us together.

And no one could take that away from us.

I believed for so long that l deserved to be alone. That's always the way my life seemed to go with people. Maybe that's why I had such faith in God — faith in something other — as I always felt their presence. Even at my lowest point, my faith always stayed in my head and heart. It meant the world to have this support, this friendship with faith that stayed with me, even when I tried so hard to push it away.

When the tests were finished, and Darragh was diagnosed with Cerebral Palsy, I turned to faith once more for the strength to get through this. It was just one of those things that can happen, I thought to myself, and it wouldn't happen again to any other children we may decide to have. This is what I told myself.

Honestly, I didn't believe some of the medical professionals. I couldn't shake the voice in my head that debated the result, the one that told me this wasn't right - that it wasn't really Cerebral Palsy but something else completely. I remember there were so many thoughts and conflicting emotions. Why am I fighting this diagnosis? Should I not commit myself now to making this better? Why am I so convinced that this isn't right? Who is this helping?

Darragh was different in many ways, but not in the way they were saying. The illness, in my mind, went deeper inside, and not on the outside where they were looking. I just felt it wasn't as simple to find as they thought it was. My 'knowing', or so I'd come to call it, was something I trusted and I trusted it now, too. Clairsentience is the ability to receive intuitive messages via feeling, or physical sensations. To some people, this might translate as just intuition, or as an empathic connection to the world — Nonetheless, I had a strong sense that there was more to come.

The day came for Darragh and I to go home. The tests were finally completed and they had seemingly found out what was wrong. Was this it? I just wanted to go home and begin to rebuild, to somehow find solid ground and start rebuilding my world, and my son's world. I thought of all of this as we sat there preparing to leave when the doctor came to see me. They told me that something had changed. They now believed that Darragh did not have cerebral palsy. I felt such relief, and yet it only lasted for a moment. My lungs filled with lead as she looked at me and stated that it was 'something else'. She calmly told us that they couldn't let us go home — not until another specialist had seen Darragh.

In the middle of all this, all the not knowing and things changing every time we thought we were finally finding our way — I called on faith to give me courage, to face this new revelation and whatever might come. It was explained that tests would have to be completed. The results, they said, would be sent abroad and the findings would not be known for up to six months. They told us that a muscle biopsy and bloods would have to be done. We would be placed on a waiting list, but what I didn't know then was that the tests they wanted to do were very expensive and not covered here in Ireland. It wasn't really a waiting list we were on, it was more a case of waiting for funds to be released in order for the tests to be carried out.

I looked at my little boy, wishing I could tell him that it would all be fine, that it could finally be over. Still, the hospital visits continued. We mainly saw Darragh's kidney specialist. Sometimes, we were called to have other small tests done. They couldn't find what they were looking for but they had markers for what they thought it was. Darragh's liver and kidneys were not working properly, we learned, and yet not once were Gerry and I told what they were specifically looking for. They wanted to have the 'big picture' — all the results together. By now, a lot of time had passed. Darragh was three years old. Not knowing left me feeling very lost and terrified, and all this time I had one thought as I prayed.

"What are they looking for? And how bad was this going to be?"

Life, in the meantime, went on and we did what we could to find a rhythm with this new struggle very much at the forefront of our thinking. We were living in hope, trying to convince ourselves that, somehow, this was all a huge mistake.

Things like this don't happen to us.

That's what everyone tells themselves. People rule themselves out of all kinds of misfortune; car crashes, hiking accidents, cancer and all the rest of it. You put everything you fear in a box, you label it and distance yourself from it in the hopes that it'll never find you. But that's not how it plays out for any of us. And when that thing that you dread, that thing you never even imagined yourself waking up finally happens, it takes time to get your head around it all — that it's all real and this is what life looks like now.

Time is, as is often repeated, a great healer but in the meantime, it just wasn't happening on my time. I needed help, I needed faith and some form of hope to pave the way from here to healing, and for that I needed something bigger than myself. I looked upwards and asked for whatever God was willing to give to get me through this. And in return, I was given light — a peace and a hope that surrounded me, that made me more at ease with the world, and in all of it I felt protected and loved. That was my armour.

Eventually, we got word that Darragh was to have his tests. They did a muscle biopsy and gave us the news that we now faced yet another six-month wait before any results would arrive. Six more months of not knowing.

How do you function through the uncertainty and all the chaos as a family? We had other children that needed our time, our care, and our energy. The 'how' was beyond us for a time, but we needed to be there for them. All of them. The 'how' would come with time, but for now, we knew we would just have to move forward with one foot in front of another. It was our role as parents to keep going despite the lows and the cloud that hung over us. And still, even in the face of that, we persevered for Darragh, and for our family.

It was during this time as we waited on results that we became pregnant with our son, Sean. It was in our minds that we ought to try and live as fully as we could and with our hearts open. We believed that nothing deserved the right to close our hearts to the world. Together, Gerry and I decided that we would try to live a normal life and to allow what was coming to come. Stress served no one. We made up our minds to find happiness where we could, to have faith, and to look forward to the birth of our baby. And that's exactly what we did.

CHAPTER FIVE
WHEN ALL HELL COMES KNOCKING

———•+•———

As it turns out, Darragh's world was one we were not even remotely prepared for. Our first dose of bad news was that he had something they called Mitochondrial disease. The doctor sat there, burdened by the weight of bad news.

He held his head in his hands as he looked at us, or, perhaps through us.

"I can't cure this," he said. "This is a lifelong disease."

They had so little information, and everything they knew

filled us with fear —and still, they said, more tests were to be done before anything could be explored. Months went by and Darragh had started school.

We began to grow worried as he was beginning to show signs of difficulty both with others and in the classroom. We were also searching everywhere for any information about mitochondrial disease but there was so little to be found. By this time, Sean had also come into the world, full of laughter and adding so much warmth to that time. And still, the journey that now lay ahead of Darragh was always in our mind.

I'll never forget the particular day we went in for the results. We were shown into the room and we noticed there was a box of tissues sitting right in front of us on the table. We knew that whatever was coming was going to be big. We were hit so hard when we were told Darragh had mitochondrial disease, but knowing that there was something else was too much to bear. They calmly and quietly told us that Darragh had been diagnosed with autism. This meant lots of new appointments for him; hospital visits, physiotherapists, occupational therapists and speech therapists. By now, The hospital staff in the wards now knew both Darragh and I very well. It wasn't a great thing but in some ways it was comforting. We weren't walking into the unknown, or so it felt. These people knew our names, and they wanted to help. This made it easier for Darragh as he didn't handle change well. He had also long begun to have meltdowns when he was faced with something different or new, and this was something we were still learning about with him.

At this time, we had decided to move house, which might seem odd. Things, at the time, were picking up financially and we felt a fresh start would help. We also began to realize that our family had grown quite large. We were now in a position to buy our own home, and so we bought a large four bedroom house in Westmeath and we moved in on Christmas Eve. It was to be our new start. My three eldest children were not too thrilled with the idea of moving away from their friends, while Adam and Darragh were still too young to remember. It was New Year's Day when Gerry got a call from the people he worked with. Everything had dried up, they said; they no longer had work. We had just 'owned' our house for a little over a week.

We had our follow up appointments with our kidney specialist; a kind man who knew Darragh since he was six weeks old. On this particular visit, my mother and my children were with me and I was now heavily pregnant once more with Gerry and I's fourth child. He told me that he had been told about the mitochondrial diagnosis and mentioned that he would do what he could to help. I then asked if he could look at my youngest son, Sean, as I had concerns that Sean was starting to become delayed in his development and not doing things as he ought to have been doing for his age. He was surprised to know that there were no tests being done for my son Sean for the same disease.

I was in shock. I hardly knew anything about Darragh's condition, and least of all that it could be genetic. I didn't think that Sean might have it too. I asked the doctor for his opinion on the matter, and I remember the look on his face; a look I knew all too well — the same look that the nurses and doctors gave me when I was first told about Darragh. He confirmed my worst fears and told me that Sean would also have it, and even worse, my unborn daughter would too. He had asked if myself and Gerry had been told that this was genetic? No one had told us. I then questioned him on our other children; none of whom had mitochondrial disease.

He explained that Gerry and I were not 'compatible' and that this would have to be looked into.

I have never felt such devastation. I felt so absolutely overwhelmed with distress that my strength almost left me entirely, but after processing what we were told, I knew I would never change a thing. I could never be without my children. I wondered then how my unborn baby was going to be affected. My heart ached so many times with the thought of it, but the one thing I was sure of was that though she hadn't even been born yet, that we would never love her any less, not for a second.

When the next appointment came, I knew that I had to ask about Sean and my unborn child whom we had named "Lisa". I knew that Gerry and I had to push for answers. The doctor came in as soon as we were seated, and he was greeted by our anger. I asked immediately to have Sean examined, which he agreed to do so. He also wanted to do further tests on Darragh, explaining that Sean, too, ought to go through the same tests to see if he could get any more answers. Until then, and until the results were gotten, nothing could be confirmed. In the six weeks that followed, Sean was becoming more delayed in his development. He quickly became worse than Darragh.

His understanding of language was poor and he wasn't speaking at all. Not a single word. He was a very content child, but it felt like nothing held any meaning for him; he was living entirely in his own world. For the longest time, he couldn't even walk or stand, but he never stopped smiling.

Aine, Ryan, Erica, Aaron, Amy

When the results finally returned, our fears were made real; Sean had mitochondrial disease. The hospital also wanted to perform an MRI scan of Sean's brain to see if he had suffered any brain damage.

I was told that there was a 1% to 5% chance that Sean could die in the machine. It might be a low percentage to some, but I refused to take any chances on my son's life no matter how big or small they might be. They found the disease in the results of Sean's blood tests, as it turns out, rather than through a muscle biopsy like they had to do with Darragh. But this also meant that the condition was affecting Sean in different ways. Now, with every child we had, the symptoms of the disease were getting worse. Eventually, with further tests, Sean was also later diagnosed with autism, and it was a lot worse than Darragh's. Soon, Sean started to fall far behind in school until the difference between him and the children of his same age group became too large to overlook. He needed help.

Our time in Westmeath was a time of great uncertainty. We were still learning about this thing called mitochondrial disease that had forever changed our lives, and at the same time, coping with autism. All the while, Gerry managed to find work where he could, and finally, when our financial circumstances began to sink into the red, it was my mother who gave us the line we needed to get back up again. We stayed there for just under four years; four years of scrimping and trying to make ends meet. And on top of all this, we were unable to pay our mortgage.

Somehow, even as we were finding it difficult to find Sean the supports he needed, even as their conditions continued to grow and change, we managed to keep it all together. We had each other and that was all that mattered. Our family, our parents and our siblings; Sharon, Ciaran, Eamon and Wayne — they were our pillars of strength; our light at the end of a very dark tunnel.

CHAPTER SIX
DARRAGH — THE WIZ

—•—

W hen you have met one child with autism, you have met only one child with autism as each child differs in each and every way. They are all unique and have their own little quirks. This was something we learned over time. In the beginning, however, Darragh had set up expectations for everything that had not yet happened; expectations that we would spend the next decade unlearning as we learned more about Sean and Lisa. Whatever we knew in the beginning

— about autism, about mitochondrial disease — we knew from Darragh.

There are a few things that make Darragh different, starting with the fact that he knows he's autistic. He is keenly aware of it and understands what it means. He struggles to interact with people, or with ordering food, fearing that they won't understand him, or that they can't relate to what he's saying. He is paralyzed by the thought that people are judging him without saying it out loud. Even stranger is that he is almost an adult in a child's body — so that he almost doesn't even know how to interact with other children because of the gap in maturity that exists between them, strange as that sounds. He is verbal, and he communicates his needs; something that made a world of difference.

As he grew up, we found that he had developed a serious personality, and yet, that he could also be very bubbly and, at times, full of energy. This also painted his condition. He gets upset, and there are things that bother him that we were never prepared for — and still, his ability to work with us is an enormous thing that we have never taken for granted. What we didn't know then was that he is on the spectrum on a different level due to his P.D.D.N.O.S., or, Persuasive Developmental Disorder

Not Otherwise Specified. And that this mattered a great deal.

I remember the first time he shut off from the world — his face changed and we didn't recognize what it meant, only that it was different, and that something was wrong. He left the room, and wandered off into a quiet place. We learned to recognize that this is how he copes. There are signs; elements of his personality and his particular way of thinking that tell us things. He flaps his hands when he's excited, or sometimes when he's upset about something and it's up to us to work out which is which. He needs time to organize his thoughts and becomes frustrated if we ask him to make decisions without giving him time to think. At times, when he struggles to explain his thoughts, his frustrations will show themselves on his face, and he eventually leaves the room — and you have to go after him, to pry it from him. He tries to hide it, to not tell you things; to keep it to himself. Even though he does not present with as many obvious traits as his siblings, his routine still has to be repetitive for him to be secure.

And then there's his relationship with others. He is extremely anti-social, and his ability to deal with people is deeply affected. He doesn't know how to take people if they're joking; he just doesn't get it. And worse, still — he gets upset if he thinks you're laughing at him. Meanwhile, at school, Darragh can be a loner. He won't get involved with others and he tries so hard to stay in the background, to not be noticed if he can get away with it. Even a conversation with Darragh can take a long time, he will stop you mid-sentence to analyse what has been said and to be reassured that he understands it. He is so much more mature in many ways which prevents interaction with most children his own age. Despite this, he luckily has a few close friends.

It's often been asked where autism comes from, and why the minds of autistic children struggle with such complex problems. However, there is also a growing conversation that surrounds the nature of the thing itself and whether autism is, at the end of all things, a purely debilitating condition.

It's very common, we've since learned, that children with autism have extraordinary skills; skills that present themselves at a young age, and at a level that ought to be far beyond their age. Darragh was no exception. As he grew older and developed interest in the wider world, we found, to our surprise, that Darragh had an incredible interest in computers. It's true that in today's world, more and more children are growing up with smartphones, tablets and laptops — connecting them with an unlimited amount of information in a way we never had.

It's a world where children can be given a question and find the answer in ten second or less. They learn, and as they've grown up with these things not knowing any different, it's become a part of their learning, and a part of their knowledge; their skillset. And still, Darragh was on a whole other level.

Darragh is an absolute whiz around laptops in ways that we barely understand. It made itself known the day our eldest son, Dean, came home from college where he was studying software development and found that Darragh had an extraordinary understanding of that same material that he'd just been working with that day. We discovered that Darragh could create programmes. It barely made sense to us. Dean had learned how to code in university, and he took great pride in learning to do so — and so you can imagine how hard it was for him, and for us, to believe that here was this boy who had tucked himself away in his space and somehow found a way to teach himself — he had taught himself how to code.

It had become his escape. This is how Darragh learned to cope.

When Darragh became stressed, he wrote code. The effect was immediate. It transforms him. The stress disappears and he enters his own world, becoming hyperfocused on the task in front of him. This only grew as he became older until one day, it developed to an entirely new level. Darragh loved to game, you see — but Darragh had a problem. And in order to fix this problem, he came up with a solution. He created a website; one where people could come and talk and share their love for this space game that he loved so much. And then came a second problem. Darragh, being a child, had no time to oversee this website that grew larger and busier with every passing day — and this he also solved. He did this by way of one day writing out a set of questions on a clipboard and then interviewing candidates.

The successful ones became site moderators — and not one of them knew that Darragh was a boy; a boy who had learned to code, to build websites, and to utilize people as resources to solve his problems. 20 people were interviewed, and from this group, three were chosen to take on this task. Eventually, Darragh grew tired of this website and now no longer uses it. As it turns out, the website still exists and continues to be moderated to this day.

Then comes the obvious problem.

Our child had placed an advert on a popular forum and had hired — actually *hired* — strangers. We had always thought our boy to be someone in need of our help, and now he was solving adult problems with incredibly complex adult solutions. It was then that we realized that this was so much more than we had ever imagined, and that it was now our turn, as parents, to catch up with our son.

CHAPTER SEVEN

SEAN — THE ARTIST

‑‑‑ ‑‑ ‑‑‑

We are always in danger of having too much confidence in labels. We use them for everything — for relationships and states of mind, and particularly — for conditions and diseases. What comes of that is a habit of tarring everyone with the same brush, painting them with the same traits, the same problems, and the same personalities. Sean is, however, evidence that autism is much more complex than any one label can accurately cover. Put simply, not every case is the same; it's not a descriptive label that tells you everything about a child.

There is so much in him that is different from the others both in terms of personality and how he deals with sensory information — not least the fact that he also has additional needs. But at the heart of it all; he's a boy who is capable of great talent and remarkable achievements. It's also true that Sean finds difficulty in doing what's asked of him. It's true that, although he is a very bubbly child, that he cannot deal with crowds of people or with noises. This doesn't define him, even if it defines a great deal of what we have to do each day to give him a quality of life. Life becomes a series of tasks in this way, and the objective is the ability for us to function as a family from day-to-day.

There are things that you might never think of; like going to the cinema. With each visit, we have to bring a pair of headphones which he uses to block out a great deal of sensory information. Without these, Sean becomes upset until he eventually lets out steam in the form of an emotional outburst, and in those times, our only choice is to leave. We can never leave him alone. This is both because of how he react to the world around him, and due to his lack of awareness of danger; you can't turn your back on him for even one second. And in doing so, you might turn around to find that Sean is simply gone. And then you have a problem.

Every day is filled with endless routine. He gets up and sits with his iPad followed by two slices of bread with butter and a drink. He will then sit down with all of his SpongeBob toys beside him in a row. They are all lined up according to size from smallest to biggest, and they each have a special place where they will sit. He puts his uniform on — which has to be on the same chair every day; his coat on the same chair; his schoolbag beside the backdoor. He has to know where he is going and what he will be doing that day. If he says something to you he will say it over and over until you repeat it back to him. And be prepared to answer him as he won't leave the room until you do. He watches the same things on TV, over and over without ever getting tired of them; all of which are recorded for him. He can say all of the lines and pauses it to repeat the words. He doesn't like the blinds in the living room to be opened and before he gets home from school we make sure they're closed. He likes to put on his pyjamas as soon as he gets home and he will sit in the same spot for hours on end. He only likes to have baths and does not like getting his hair cut. We even go so far as preparing the exact same dinner each and every day, as he will not eat anything else. Ever.

Simply put: Sean will have a loud and complete meltdown if you so much as stick a toe beyond his usual routine. He cannot handle it, and you cannot change a single thing. And each weekend, we have to do the same things, in the same order — as if at some undetermined point, our lives became stuck on a never-ending loop.

One big endless, happy routine.

Imagine, if you like, that the average child's mind is a maze — a great set of walls, and them; tiny little things that get a thrill from chaos and disorder. Now, in order for you to navigate that maze, you must make sense of that disorder, and find a path through the chaos in order to understand your child. When it comes to Sean and his autism, the walls are mirrored, so that after a time, what you think is the answer is really just a reflection of your logic. Simply put: autism does not work by your logic.

And to even begin to try and understand it, you have to abandon the idea that your way of thinking will connect with their way of thinking.

Sean silently and peacefully expresses his anger with his face. This is one of our cues. And yet, he also uses his emotions to make you give him what he wants. Before you've even said no to one of Sean's demands, he'll work himself into an upset so that you say yes. For this to happen, we've learned, Sean must have an awareness of the situation — of how we see him. He knows he's autistic, although he doesn't understand the word. He doesn't like being called autistic, either, because he thinks he's being called a bad name. He knows that he's different, and that is something that we're always aware of. We have come to understand that there are an endless list of things that can sink a hook into our son's emotional stability and take it for a ride. Among these is the fact that Sean wants to be everyone's friend. He's so full of enthusiasm that he truly believes that the moment he meets you, that he's your best friend. However, it's not in the interest of every child to be friends with a child who fundamentally doesn't understand the words over and under when searching for a ball, or a child who believes that everything is free game. He believes that he can take what he wants, as he doesn't understand the concept of ownership. Yours and mine are words that don't exist in Sean's vocabulary. Moreover, Sean exists on the wavelength of a five year old child making all of this far more difficult than it has any right to be for a child of 10. Naturally, this causes him to get very upset.

There is still so much we don't understand about Sean, and yet, there are also things that bring us, and him, a great deal of joy. There is nothing that fascinates him so much as making videos and drawing. If he likes something, he can draw it. He draws things that are real — things that we haven't seen. Our children each possess a memory that astounds us, and in Sean, it manifests as the ability to remember things which he can later put to paper in extraordinary detail. Their memories are put to the test in ways we never expected. There was the time we discovered that, having taken a liking to watching Korean shows in English, which he would watch with Korean subtitles, he had gone and recorded a personal introduction entirely in Korean. Just as Darragh had committed himself to code, Sean found a talent in languages and in visual imagery.

Though there are few days that give us a sense of progress — our family outing to Tayto Park was certainly one of them. It is my idea of a nightmare to take these children into the middle of vast, noisy, unpredictable crowds in a loud and bright environment packed with sensory information and a thousand things that our children might want. There is — with Sean — one great danger of which we're always aware. He is capable of extraordinary hyperfocus, and it's because of this that he can commit himself to a task and excel in it. However, it's also a dangerous element of his personality. In this instance, it became a problem when Sean decided that he wanted a teddy. It's not enough to say that he wanted it — he *needed* it.

Amy, immediately seeing the danger, said no and that no one can win it. And yet this was an attempt to meet his logic with her logic. And his logic, in his mind, always won. With every step they took in the opposite direction, Sean's voice grew louder.

"I can win it!"

In the end, there was no choice but to try. Despite efforts to persuade him to let someone else try, he would allow no one to win it for him. And though we might have stayed there until the end of time, until the teddy had been bought and paid for ten times over, Sean won that teddy on the second try and proudly held it up for everyone to see. In the end, not one of them would get on a single ride, because this was not a fairground in which our autistic children were hopelessly lost — but their playground; their world in which their logic was king; a place where their will reigned supreme. And for us to see them in that way, being themselves in a place where so much life threatened to undo them at the seams, we found that they could enjoy themselves, and even *thrive*. And that meant everything.

PART II
YOU KEEP ON LIVING

CHAPTER EIGHT

LISA, THE LYRICAL

———

I'd like to say that Lisa has always been different. But that's not really true. Lisa was born on September 27th, 2009, and entered the world quite quickly. When she arrived, they were forced to give her oxygen as her colouring was entirely wrong. That night, as I held her, her lips turned blue. The nurses took her to the doctor where she stayed for an hour and a half, as a precautionary measure they said. I was so worried that I couldn't sleep. I just lay there staring at her. She did, in the end, recover and they allowed us to take her home. For Amy, who wanted a sister so badly, and for all of us, she was the greatest joy. In all our photos, she plays and laughs and rolls around with all the madness of a child. She was adventurous; playful; vocal, even. She even taught her older brother, Sean, how to say 'Mama' and 'Dada.' What strikes us as strange now in later years, however, is the energy and the awareness in her eyes. It's as if she saw the whole world around her then — really saw it. She had an awareness of her surroundings and she looked at us — *at* us, instead of looking past us, or through us as it eventually came to be. Lisa played with the other children and enjoyed her food and was, in every way that she could be, a normal child.

Amy and Erica

One day, sometime after Lisa's 2nd birthday — something changed. Suddenly, the photos were different. The Lisa we saw in our photos was now different, quiet, and distant. It was as if something had clicked in her mind and transformed her entire awareness of the world — and you could see it. It was clear to see in her eyes. There was an energy once in them that we could no longer see, an awareness that she no longer seemed to have.

We were told, as we had come to expect, that Lisa also had mitochondrial disease. Up until now, like the others, she had gone through a series of tests. Her health, nonetheless, became problematic more quickly than any of the others. Her heart began to give her issues, and it was decided by her doctors that she required surgery. A muscle biopsy was carried out along with an echocardiogram on her heart as the doctor had to ensure that she was well enough to go under anaesthesia for her operation. At this time, they detected a heart murmur when they listened to Lisa's heart. This was something new and much to my dismay, as another health problem meant another doctor, more tests, more questions and more waiting.

Lisa, we were told, had what is called a floppy tube, and when it comes to children with mitochondrial disease, this issue doesn't fix itself as is possible for a healthy child. We now had another doctor to add to our long list of doctors and specialists which now included three specialists, two physiotherapists, two occupational therapists and two speech therapists. Furthermore, these were to become a set multiplied by three for each of my children. A week after we left the hospital, Lisa was diagnosed with autism and we came to learn that she was completely nonverbal. Lisa was, by far, the earliest to be diagnosed and is an unusual case in that she was diagnosed at the age of two which was a lot earlier than doctors would normally diagnose a child with autism at the time. What was also interesting about her case was that, up until a certain point, she had been displaying normal childhood development and behaviour until everything changed.

We have learned in life, and from having three children with autism, that some of the easier, old fashioned ways work best when making life more simple. And toilet training was no exception. We had been trying to toilet train Lisa for a while and, between the school and ourselves, we could neither find an easy way nor any way at all, as she was not co-operating. The first thing we decided to use was an old toilet support as it has a handle on each side. Lisa immediately felt more secure, but that wasn't enough as she still wouldn't go to the toilet. So with great thought, we came to realize that security was the issue and that her nappy was obviously her safety blanket. So we came up with the idea of leaving her nappy on and cutting the underneath out so that she still felt like she had her nappy on. This worked like a charm. When she went, we all gave her praise and said hooray and made such a big deal of the whole thing that Lisa thought that this was absolutely great. Change is a massive ordeal for these children, and believing that she had her nappy on, having that security — that made all the difference.

Among her many struggles, Lisa also suffers from kidney infections. She's tall and big for her age, and all of this became a problem when the tests began and the doctors demanded things from us that seemed impossible. How do you take a sample from a difficult and unpredictable child who refuses to sit still? She was too big for the bags that the doctors use to get samples from young children. There simply weren't any answers for Lisa, so we were forced to come up with our own. Gerry and I thought for days before we realized that she wouldn't sit on the toilet without the toilet support, so we had to think up a good way to get a sample that was still sterilized while also keeping Lisa's difficulties in mind. Eventually, we came up with a plan. We got a plastic bowl and sterilized it with Milton and hot water and we put the bowl in to the toilet. When we took the bowl out, in order to keep her sample sterilized, we used a syringe, which we had also sterilized, to remove the sample and put it in a jar. And like that, we'd found a way to get around the issue when it seemed as though we never would.

As of now, at the age of 9, she continues to do things a three-year-old would do, and we still have to find creative ways to deal with new problems. She has no sense of danger at all. I have to lock all doors, make sure there is nothing small on the floor as everything goes straight in her mouth. And despite being very tall, she still likes to sit on your knee like a baby would. Like the others, she also likes routine and cannot, in any way, handle change.

CHAPTER NINE
A LEARNING PROCESS

———•———

A s she grew, Gerry and I came to find that Lisa wakes up between two and four in the morning most mornings — putting a great amount of strain on both of us as parents. Managing seven children, and with Sean and Darragh being difficult to manage, made being a parent so much more exhausting than it ought to be. Now, as Lisa began to grow more distant, as she became unpredictable and restless, we grew more exhausted, and the effort to get through a day became so much more costly. Our lives had once again gone through a new change; one that meant that we were no longer going to get very much sleep.

She began to fling our bedroom door open, just standing there looking at us, flapping her hand. If you don't turn around to her straight away she'll sometimes come over and stick her finger in your eye, or she'll take your hand and try to pull you. Sometimes, she'll go into the sitting room, sit on the chair in the dark and put the remote beside her as she still doesn't know how to use it. And regardless of the time, she will wait for you to come in and turn it on for her, and she will not go back to sleep until you've turned it on. My husband, Gerry, mainly stays with her when she wakes, having no choice but to accept exhaustion as she mostly listens to him.

She will have a lot of meltdowns and you won't know what happened, or even why. It might be as simple as a noise on the TV, or something that may have fallen on the floor. She becomes difficult when having a meltdown and this can go on for hours. It's upsetting for each of us, for both her parents and the rest of the family to watch her in this state. In that moment, it's up to myself or my husband to sit with Lisa until it ends. We hug her tight, doing everything we can to ease her back into a calm state, and still she'll try to hit you while also not wanting you to leave. The moment you leave her in that state, whether you try to leave the room or just a few feet away, she'll pull your hand and draw you back towards her, to sit with her, to give her comfort. And when she's finally able to compose herself again, it's like it never happened. It just repeats, and each time, you can only sit and hold her until it ends.

Our lives are anything but normal because of all this. Gerry and I barely ever sleep in the same bed. It's lucky that we have such a good and solid relationship, and that things still work for us. Dealing with all of this, it takes a kind of determination that is put to the test every single day, and only by working together is it made a bit easier.

We started to look at ways that we could help Lisa, to Lisa-proof the house and organize a system that would make things a little more manageable. We started locking the kitchen door and closing the stair gate. The bathroom door must be locked or we would regularly have floods with Lisa being fond of turning on the taps and leaving the room. And like the others, there is a great deal of routine. Lisa still has a bottle last thing at night and first thing in the morning. She will not drink out of anything unless it has a bottle top or a sports cap. She will eat the same dinner every day and likes to watch TV. She hasn't got any interest in any toys at all. She does like books, however. She wanders up and down the hall and into each room all day, turning on all of the lights as she goes along while opening and closing doors.

In the years since, though Lisa lives in a world of her own, we've learned that she isn't unaware. She interacts with us, she will give us a hug and a kiss. We've begun to see the warmth and the creativity beneath the things that give her problems. She loves it when you're singing to her no matter how bad at singing you might be. This was one of our favourite discoveries — that Lisa is a huge fan of music. It's our belief that she understands music better than anything else, and that she'll likely grow to interact with it even more in the future.

We've worked hard to find things that soothe her; her lava lamp; a weighted blanket that gives her a sense of security; and particularly her bean bag. But all of these things are hers. Singing, however, was something that brought us closer.

I remember sitting in the bath, singing her a song and watching as she listened and began to laugh at my singing voice. I didn't even care. All that mattered was that she listened, that she found something in it that soothed her, and she responded. She saw me. And these are the moments that we live for.

CHAPTER TEN
FROM MY EYES TO HERS

———•+•———

When I look at my daughter Lisa, all I see is her truth, what she wishes she could say in words. Instead, she does it with her smile, her eyes, her tears, and her hands — always guiding me. She may not speak the words, but everything in her beautiful face talks to me without words. Her actions speak to me, and over time, I've learned to make sense of them, to understand the meaning under the surface. Lisa's face will tell a million stories without ever speaking a single word. And while I never completely go into Lisa's world with her, she can at least take me some of the way so that I can see the messages she leaves at the door. And all the things it might take to get there might feel silly, but to Lisa, to children with autism, it's perfectly normal. So take the leap and just go.

There's so much peace in getting to sit with your child and finding an understanding with them. A bad day is a bad day no matter what way you look at it, and it's no different for any of us when we're stressed or going through something negative. They want to escape that stress, to connect with someone who can help them. So you ask yourself: How do I cope with bad moments? What do I do to feel calm again?

You do whatever it takes. Sing, if it helps, and dance until you get tired. Flap your arms if you need to, because these things make them feel better, and at the end of it all, you're just as likely to feel better yourself. So much of their world is different, and yet very much the same underneath. During a meltdown, when they cry or thrash, they're just trying to tell you something — to communicate in the only way they know how. One of the greatest wrongs you can do is to treat your child as if they are different, because then they will act and feel different, and this might seem difficult to believe at first. When the room is quiet, Lisa sits in her favourite chair with her tablet, switching from programme to programme, and always the same ones in different languages. Then, when the noise starts to fade into silence, her hands start to flap, and the screaming and crying begins. You often think to yourself: "What happened in those five seconds, what changed?"

The room is still the same, and nothing has moved, and nobody entered; this is according to our logic. But to my autistic daughter, something changed in that five second window; a vanishing noise; a changing colour; an unusual sound; all and any of these can set Lisa off. It's so often a sensory thing, something that isn't immediately obvious to us, but to Lisa it's very upsetting and challenging. So where do you go with that? It's always our first instinct in times of trouble to wear our emotions on our face. Everyone gets visibly stressed or muddled up.

Sometimes you swear and sometimes you close your eyes and ball up your emotions to try and get a hold of the situation. And when we act differently, with anger or with stress, this makes every meltdown worse. Our children can feel our fear, so if they think that we don't know what to do, that we're afraid, or stressed, or confused, then they'll begin to channel that same emotion. All the fear that we carry around with us eventually makes its way into the minds of our autistic children; a fear of going to the shop, a fear of going out, a fear of a meltdown happening when we're out — it's all these fears that so often lead to our children's meltdowns. They recognize something in us, and they react. We need to believe that it's going to be okay, and we need to believe in ourselves. Our reality, and our children's reality aren't so different. We just have a knack of labelling things, and when we label something, we expect it to do what it says on the label; that's where our problems begin. Labels are dangerous things; they change your perspective, how you look at things. You start looking at them as something other, something foreign, something you can't understand.

The problem is that if you start to think in this way, then you'll begin to believe that they're beyond your understanding, and nothing could be further from the truth. In the same way that we look at ourselves, or our other children, we know that we are all different, and that no two people are the same — but we have much more in common than not. We've since learned that in the moment, labels don't help. Calm helps, self-preservation and self-control helps, and owning our own thoughts helps; these are the things that serve you. If we expect our children to act in a certain way, they will oblige us. But if we look at things positively, and act as we wish them to act, then things will begin to change, even if only in subtle ways in the beginning. So just learn to be in the moment, to see them as you see yourself, instead of trying to label it and then act accordingly.

Our daughter, Lisa, is an amazing human being. You walk into a room and stand in front of her, and she'll look at you, but she has no words. You say 'hi' and she will smile at you, or sometimes look at you with a blank look on her face, which is just her way. But the one thing you'll get from her is acceptance. She doesn't judge you, she never thinks in terms of what this person wants from me, she takes you for what you are and who you are, as the person who's standing right in front of her. She doesn't care if you like her or don't like her, and she is capable of so much love. This really and truly is the beautiful person she was created to be, if only trapped in a body that limits her expression — and still she finds a way. Lisa will take your hand like she's known you all her life. She'll bring you to what she needs, or where she needs to go to show you what she wants because she feels safe with you even though your ability to communicate is so limited. There is absolutely no judgement. She doesn't like lots of noise, yet she can be the noisiest person in the room when she's comfortable. She loves colours of all types and loves to be outside in nature all the time; she loves life in every way — all of life and everyone in it.

When you look at Lisa, your first instinct might be to label her as different, as someone who lacks something that you don't. But when you look into Lisa's eyes, you can see all the same things that make people beautiful; all of the things we love and admire in people. And wouldn't it be so wonderful if we could all live our lives from the same perspective as a child with autism? Lisa will always have her ups and downs, her chaotic days and her meltdowns, and yet right after they pass, she goes on with life as if they never happened. Her struggle is so great and still she finds it in herself to carry on loving. At every point in life, we need to see the bad days as Lisa does; not as a hopeless ending but as just that; a bad day.

CHAPTER ELEVEN
A GUIDE TO NAVIGATING MELTDOWNS

—•—

There's a great deal you learn to accept when you become a mother to children with autism. You can limit the difficult episodes, and with some creative thinking, you can even avoid them at times, and then there is the fact — that autism often makes its own rules, and that you can't do much more than be there and use all the tools at your disposal to deal with the episodes when they happen. Of course, it's not right to say that you're powerless; there are often signs to warn you in advance.

Sometimes, when Lisa comes home from school, she can be very happy, almost as if she's on a high, so to speak. When she's like this, we know straight away that there's a meltdown coming. This might seem a little strange as it runs counter to logic, but behind it is a logic that is just as true — that, as it is with gravity, and as we have discovered with our children; what goes up must come down.

As the evening goes by, Lisa starts to come down from her high and immediately shifts to a different gear. First comes the crying, followed with banging her head on the pillow. Most of the time we try to distract her by talking to her, or we'll put her into her room where we'll play her music. Sensory aids are always massively helpful in these scenarios. She typically continues to hit her head off the pillow but we know that she is, in her room at least, safe from harm as we removed everything that she could use to hurt herself. It was this thought that gave us an idea. What would happen if, in such a state, Lisa decided that she wanted to stumble out of her room and down the stairs? Or if she were to go into a kitchen full of utensils whose purpose she barely understands? It was my father who came up with a solution for the problem. He came up with a gate that you could easily slip into place outside the door. On the door is a lock which cannot be opened. This allows us to put Lisa in the room with her bedroom door open, knowing that she can't get out and cause harm to herself or to others. The good thing about this gate is that it can be expanded for purpose even as your kids grow taller.

In her safe, familiar place, and with her music to soothe her, Lisa starts to calm down. When she finishes, she stands at the gate looking for you to let her out. We've found, also depending on where your child is when a meltdown happens can influence the outcome, when Lisa is sitting on a chair or on the living room sofa and a meltdown occurs, we can get behind her and give her a bear hug. During this time, we hold her arms while we're giving her a hug, and as a result of being behind her, she can't hit or bite you. Moreover, children with autism like security and being held in a tight embrace as it gives them a great deal of comfort. This can most easily be seen when Lisa uses her weighted blanket. For her, security and feeling safe is such a big part of her life.

A great deal of the time has to be spend in developing creative new ways to deal with Lisa and her meltdowns, as they are often unpredictable and frequently leave us exhausted. But we also get tired of having to be inventive. For the average parent, there's a measure of bliss to be had on a long, tiring day in just being able to follow a routine. But when the source of those long, tiring days is your daughter's episodic outbursts, you eventually have to face your exhaustion and find solutions. Sometimes, however, there are moments of joy that separate the long periods of keeping our heads above water.

The benefits of bringing Lisa in for a shower didn't make themselves known immediately, and we never really imagined that it would turn into something significant, and yet that's exactly what happened. Showers are something she used to not like at all like many children with autism. To get around this, I put on a pair of shorts and a t-shirt and I sit with her for as long as it takes. She loves the security of me being in there with her. She feels safe. And while she's in there I sing to her. Now, though I am not a great singer, this is all to Lisa's amusement as she thinks it's hilarious. It's quite common for Lisa to now take me by the hand and bring me in to have a shower. And it was as a result of this that a more recent fond memory emerged that reminded us of the humanity in our children, and their ability to make us laugh. One day, I brought Lisa in for a shower, taking all the steps as normal and singing to her all the while. From the shower, I remember I could hear a noise in the hall, and soon, the noise grew louder. Before long, I realized what I was actually hearing — the wind chimes.

We had put them there as a warning when one of the children tried to open the door and get out. I immediately fell into panic mode and set into action, but this required a few steps. I wrapped Lisa in a towel, and I sat her on my bed, hoping that she'd stay still until I came back. I ran into the hall with my soaking wet t-shirt and shorts, already making this situation much more dramatic than it needed to be, to find Sean wrestling with the dog for a towel. Jamie, the assistance Labrador who would come much later, was pulling the towel one way and Sean was pulling it the other way in a savage game of tug-o-war by the door. At the same time, our little terrier Kim was biting at Sean's feet thinking that all of this was a great game.

Before I could do anything about either of these things, Sean starts gliding along the floor, being pulled along the hall by the dog as if he's on roller-skates and he thinks that this is all very funny. In an attempt to calm them, I decided to try and take the towel from the two of them, the chimes still ringing, and like that, I slipped on my butt. By this point, the towel had dropped out of the dog's mouth and out of Sean's hand, and the chimes are now hammering my eardrums. They all ran to the sitting-room. Meanwhile, recovering, I ran back into the room to find that Lisa had thrown the towel off and was now running around my bedroom — naked. She'd decided to make a sport of throwing all my stuff from the shelves onto the floor.

"Really?" I thought, standing half-exhausted and half-amused.

It all seemed so ridiculous.

My second thought, however, was a small thanks to God that this was all I had to contend with. I just sat on the bed and, in the process of drying her feet, I burst out laughing. I laughed endlessly. I laughed because of the ridiculousness of it all, because it was the only way to make sense of the often-crazy nature of our lives, and most importantly, I laughed because my children had reminded me that even autism has a bright side, and that laughter can always be found in the most unlikely of places

CHAPTER TWELVE
DEALING WITH CHANGE

———•·•———

C hange is something none of us like; certainly not as adults. We find ways to deal with change in our lives, and we move on, or we fail to accept it, and we choose to stand in that same place, fighting against the current and never getting far. Those are our choices to make. Your autistic child is no different. They fear change. They hate it. And yet their anger — the meltdowns — are nothing more than reactions inspired by the same fear, expressed in their own way. So what do you do? Change in these circumstances is something that must be handled with care. We find ways to change things without causing a meltdown. You have to take control of these situations, you need to believe it in the changes you want to make, and you need to believe in your own self and your ability to make that change real.

There is a fear that is associated with this change; some deeply held belief that it's all going to go wrong, that your child is going to react with great difficulty and drama. But it doesn't have to be that way. The drama and the chaos is an option, but not an inevitability. There is a path in getting there without the chaos, and it's not so different from how we apply change to our own lives. The key is to take it slow. Just as it is with any other person, the introduction of subtle changes are hard to notice. We start off with small things like changing something in their bedroom, and then work up to bigger things. This lesson first presented itself to us when we wanted to paint Sean's bedroom.

Consider autism and its defining traits — consider the fact that sensory information is to an autistic child ten times what it is to us. Let's imagine that your autistic child enjoys the colour blue. Each day, they come home and spend time in their room, they dress and play and wind down in that same space, and then they sleep in that same space and for all this time, the room is blue. Suddenly, your child comes home and their space is no longer blue, but red. Something has fundamentally changed, and it upsets them dramatically. Now, they cannot play in that room, they can't wind down, or play, or dress, or even sleep in that room now that the room has dramatically changed.

When we told Sean that we wanted to paint his room, he refused. Soon after, he became upset. With great effort and a lot of talking, he finally said that we could paint it with the exception that we could only paint it the same colour. It was here that we realized the potential in subtle changes. We decided when painting it to simply paint it a shade darker, not enough that anyone might easily notice, but it was undoubtedly a shade darker. Our success was marked by the fact that he didn't really notice it. Then, we started making gradual changes, day by day, like putting up shelves, and hanging things on the wall. It was essentially a process of Sean getting used to the room one day at a time, one change at a time. There were no meltdowns, and greater still is that he is now very settled in his room.

We then began to apply this same process with Lisa. We put wallpaper up on one wall of the room, and surrounded her with all her stuff. We brought her into the room, one day at a time, when there was only one or two sheets of wallpaper on the wall. We played with her in the room, and did all the things she usually does in her room each time we brought the change further along. This ensured that nothing was ever too unfamiliar, and it got easier day by day. There was only one great worry with Lisa — that being that she tends to react a week later to things instead of reacting to it at the time. Subsequently, we took our time doing up her room, and in the end, it worked out very well.

When the subtle changes began to slowly transform our lives, allowing more freedom and less chaos, we started to wonder what else could be changed, and what we might be able to achieve using the same method. And so we turned our heads to the next great obstacle; food.

This was a whole different game, as food is very much a sensory issue with children with autism. We had to start out very slow, bearing in mind that even subtle changes in food is very difficult to mask. As parents are well aware, mixing food in with the food your children usually eat is a fool's game. Children always know. This took a different approach. What we decided to do was to make a lot of different foods for each of us at dinner. The result was that Lisa started picking at everyone's plates, as that's what she does, and trying different foods. Now, after a great deal of time, Lisa eats a lot of different foods like curries, or fish, and even marshmallows and jellies which she would never have looked at before. Through everybody having something different on their plate, and knowing that she would want what was on everyone else's plate, we found success once again. We also found that putting things on different plates in the middle of the table, or leaving them on the countertop, and not forcing them on anyone, resulted in the kids taking things themselves and trying them without even being asked.

If there is one tool that has been invaluable to us —it's creativity, or in other words, thinking outside the box. When you need to deal with children who don't like to touch things that are actually very useful, like cotton wool, as a result of their texture, you have to align yourself to the idea that changing your child will only lead to failure, and the answer really lies in changing the nature of the cotton wool, without really changing anything at all. We began to wet it at first so that each one became more similar in shape and size, and my children held them until I dried them off. This was only possible because they now had a different feel and a different texture. Eventually, as all the cotton balls started to dry, the children found more similarities than differences in what they became, and that they now felt the same. Now, they will pick them up without even thinking.

Small changes matter.

We started hanging our children's coats in different places in our home, and moving the school bags to different rooms. As silly as it all might sound, our children started to accept that their things didn't have to be in a certain place all the time, and when they went to get their things it wasn't a big drama. It broke down routines and introduced a new wave of freedoms; more independence, and less overseeing.

Sometimes you forget to put a coat or a bag in the same place every day, it's hard for us parents to have to keep remembering. As a result, the benefit of these changes affected all of us — parents and children. I started out talking about how much our lives revolve around routine, how everything has its place, and when it comes to our children — that place does not change. All of this has since changed. Our children hang their coats without our help, and you can call it a small thing if you like, but parents of children with autism will find it to be a very big step in a life that's always being ruled by our child and their autism.

Though change affects our entire house, and at times, you find that guilt comes easy with change as it affects your whole family, I really feel as though the best thing we ever did for our children and the rest of our family was to take control back and find ways to make life fit with their autism rather than relying on doctors to make their autism more compatible with life. Our goal was to stop looking at our children as though each of them carried labels. We wanted them to be free of labels as much as we could allow them by giving them a sense of independence through small-yet-meaningful changes. As a result, we were able to improve not only their lives, but also our own. And these changes are possible. Remember that few specialists can tell you more about your child and who they are; nobody knows your child like you do.

CHAPTER THIRTEEN
NEW CHALLENGES
AND BIG CHANGES

—◆◆—

W e both woke up one morning, each of us agreeing in silence that something had changed. It was everywhere around us and it couldn't be ignored for much longer. That morning, we decided that if we, as a family, were to get through our situation — one that now included financial difficulties — and if we were to cope with the children's diagnoses all while still waiting on Lisa's results, we needed a change, and a big one at that. We'd long realized that this house was no longer big enough for the nine of us; the solution was in our faces. We decided that we needed to move, and it would be drastic. This time, we were going to move to Galway.

We initially wanted to move to Clare, and quickly discovered that there were very little services available for our children. The search continued for a time, and during all of this, our current reality continued to exist whether we were busy planning or otherwise. It took time, but we eventually settled on a place called Kinvara.

Initially, everything about it was hard; it was a long way away from my mother and my family, it was an entirely new place full of *change*. That alone filled us with a lot of discomfort. This was going to be hard for all of us but Kinnegad (where we were living) was only ever meant to be a short term plan. I always felt as though there was somewhere more, and that life was pulling us in a new direction. The choice was, in the end, as simple as knowing that I didn't want to rear my children in a housing estate. I needed to do this; I needed to protect them, to nurture them, to nurture their gifts. What good was Lisa's musicality, or Sean's creativity, or Darragh's understanding of code in a place like this? Moving this far away from my own family was never going to be easy, but my children had to come first.

There were complex emotions, all of them fighting against one another. Of course, I wanted to see my family, and at the same time, I felt that I had to make the break away from home; to be more independent. Gerry and I decided together that the children needed to be in a house on its own; one that was removed from dangers like busy roads and traffic; a house with its own gated garden; a place where they could be safe; a place for the children to play where we could see them all the time. They needed to be safe, but they also needed to be children.

When children with mitochondria get sick, it's not like other children who recover after a week or two. If my children get sick, they could be sick for two to three months resulting in constant visits to one doctor after another. Every year, as a family, we have to get the flu vaccination to try and prevent our children getting sick at all. It's so drastic that we were also one of the first families to get the swine flu injection when it first came into Ireland; all in an effort to compensate for how dangerous mitochondrial disease can be. I remember when they announced it on the news; swine flu. I remember the panic, and yet, for us, the panic was real. It was our worst nightmare — so much so that we were afraid to leave the house with our children because if they caught it, they had no chance of survival at all. We became hermits. And none of this was fair on our older children who were beginning to suffer as they grew older and had wants and needs of their own.

Life in all of this was not ideal for our three older children, particularly when it came to moving them so far away from their schools and friends in Westmeath. They had just settled there when we once again upturned their lives, but we felt it had to be done for their siblings. The younger children needed a chance and I knew they would re-adjust. Throughout all of this, I felt as though I was guided in my choices, as everything fell into place without a problem. We had moved within two weeks of deciding to relocate and though we had no major issues, Amy and Ryan didn't want to move and secretly, I think they believed, hoped even, that I wouldn't be able to pull the move off within two weeks. Even then, I had to be there for them, to reassure them.

When you first move, the first thing you have to do is sort out the various services needed for the children. I was told there was a team in place for our area of Kinvara, and all that was needed was the appropriate paperwork. What followed was a series of blessings: all that needed to be done was quickly done, followed by a call to the secondary school - Gort Community School. After speaking to a very helpful and kind secretary named Rena, we managed to secure a place for Ryan and Amy in the school. And then, as if it were by design, Rena also gave me names of schools suitable for Adam, Darragh and Sean. She gave me almost all of the information I needed, and when you're in the middle of such a dramatic life change, you can only be grateful for such a person, and for all the help she gave us. Straight away, the appointments for the schools were made. It all happened so fast and effortlessly.

We drove to Galway and met with Dominic Gallagher, Principal of St Joseph's National School in Kinvara. We talked for a while and the arrangements were all starting to fall into place. I told Mr Gallagher that I had a child with autism and that I needed a place for him with the aid of an SNA. He told me that if I had come to him a day later that he would have not been able to give Darragh a place in the school because the day I went in was the last day to apply for an SNA. Coincidentally, Dominic knew the Principal from my children's previous school in Kinnegad. All that he had to do was make a phone call and things were sent to him without delay. This, I felt, said it all. Only through this can I explain the feeling that surrounded that time. I felt guided, and I felt as though I had been guided here for a reason. Dominic, as it turned out, was trying to organise the opening of an autistic unit before we moved to Kinvara, but he did not have enough children to open it. The centre needed three children or more on the autistic spectrum, which I just happened to have.

St Joseph's School was to play a big role in our lives. Dominic informed us that he had been inspired to advance the unit by our intense willingness to fight for our children. With our help and the help of others, the unit was opened and Sean was to be the first and only student in the unit for one year until it was fully established. He had the best teacher you could have ever ask for in Mrs Murphy. She loved Sean very much and he adored and loved her too. She did everything in Sean's best interest, and over time, we watched him grow with the help of his teacher and the school. The unit, named Seoda, was and still is the best thing to happen to our children. With the help of an SNA named Louise and her assistance, Darragh began to do extremely well. She never left his side and throughout her work, she brought his personality to the forefront; something we will always be grateful for. Sean continues to attend Seoda with new teachers and a

SNA, and he truly loves the school.

In the end, we moved into the second house we viewed. The landlord was nice, and the house just happened to have a garden. It had everything we needed. With all the plans in place, we packed up our cars and moved all of our things. And in the end, it was all worth it.

Lisa later secured a place in a school called Rosedale; a school that caters for children like herself with severe intellectual disabilities, those with autism spectrum disorder, and physical disabilities. It is because of this school and the care provided by their teachers, their SNA team, their care staff and everybody else in the school that Lisa has grown as a person. The Principal, Breda, continues to support us in ways we are endlessly thankful for: all appointments are made through the school for Lisa, and we always get a phone call to let us know so we can be there. Beyond all this, we were now on the receiving end of some extraordinary support. Lisa began to see a paediatrician in Rosedale every few months; a woman who is now a paediatrician to all of my children as she works in the hospital they attend, and she is also aware of mitochondrial disease.

Lisa's bus picks her up every morning and drops her home in the evening and Mary and Ann, the carers on the bus, and Pat, the bus driver, care for Lisa in a way that gives us peace and fills us with thankfulness. Lisa loves them both and they go above and beyond for her. This was a time of great importance for us, and some extraordinarily good people came into our lives.

PART III
THE PATH TO SOLID GROUND

CHAPTER FOURTEEN
A NEW LIFE & THE UNEXPECTED

———•••———

Months passed and most of us were happy. The move was still fresh in our minds and everyone had settled, except for Ryan and Amy. They began to articulate, frequently, that I had moved them into the 'middle of nowhere.' However, they knew we weren't going back. We couldn't.

It took time for each of us, but after a time, they too started to settle in their new environment. They soon made friends and things changed for them both. For this to work, we needed peace, we needed to start on a strong foundation. And this peace was not the easiest thing to grasp. Still sitting in the back of our minds were the results of Lisa's muscle biopsy. We had received the mitochondrial diagnosis and we still struggled to make peace with this thing, but we still didn't have the strain which meant that we still didn't know what way this disease was going to specifically affect our children.

There are, as it turns out, a lot of strains of mitochondria and they all affect the body in different ways, and at different speeds. For example, Melas Syndrome affects the brain, nervous system and muscles. It can cause stroke-like episodes and migraines — or MERRF, which comes with a lack of voluntary coordination, epilepsy, muscle weakness and degeneration, deafness, and even dementia for some people. Ultimately, given the number of strains that exist and how each of them are different, knowing the strain is an incredibly important part of moving forward. At this point, we still had months to wait before we could find out exactly what our daughter had.

In the meantime, I became sick. It started with 'pins and needles' in my hands, and then the headaches followed. I should point out that as a mother to three autistic children, getting sick was not a luxury I could afford for very long. Despite this, it was decided that I should be sent to the hospital where I was to have an MRI of my brain. This was already becoming a problem. A week later, the phone rang. The specialist from the hospital greeted me on the other side, telling me without giving anything away that they needed to do more tests.

This was all entirely too familiar.
"What's wrong with my brain scan?" I asked.

She reluctantly held her breath. I pushed, not willing to sit and have to wait over another terrible unknown. And still, I knew that something was coming. They told me that they had found lesions on my brain. Confused, I asked what that meant. "What are you looking for?" Again, a pause. And then, "MS. We're looking for Multiple Sclerosis." In all of this, there was always one constant — and that was our ability to be present. No matter what happened, Gerry and I were always capable, even if there were days when one of us struggled, even if exhaustion brought us close to the edge of what we could do, at least we could cope.

This threatened all of that.

"Is this really happening?" I found myself saying aloud. How was I going to take care of my children? Just when things had started to move forward, just as we'd managed to lay our hands on some form of progress, the universe answers with this. First my children... and now me. It became such a weight in my mind that it threatened to create problems of its own.

I decided it was time to take a break from all of this. This was too much. There were just too many questions: What have we done to deserve this? What purpose does it serve? Why our family? And how do we move forward? There were so many answers I so desperately needed. This led me to faith. If I couldn't find the answers in front of me, then I would have to look for them elsewhere. I gave more and more time to spiritual things, and in time, people found their way onto my path; many of them spiritual people, like-minded people — and many of them helped me in ways that I needed. It was only then that I felt drawn back into a world I had left behind.

The day came for me to undergo multiple tests; tests that would go on for weeks. I had a spinal tap, a whole number of blood tests and a few nerve tests to cap it off, but the results came back with no abnormalities. The doctors couldn't understand. But I did. There was a great big weight that started to grow in my mind — a simple thought that popped its head up every time I put my mind to the task of figuring this out, and there was only one way to find out if I was right. I asked my neurologist if she could test me for mitochondrial disease. Of course, it was so far beneath the radar at that time that it wasn't even clear to them what tests were needed. She just didn't know. She would have to ring the Children's Hospital, she said. She would ask them what needed to be done. My doctor, too, had little information and didn't know much about the disease; not enough to understand what to test for, or which procedure to follow. They simply didn't have one. The Children's Hospital returned and told her to perform a muscle biopsy on my arm and leg, and then came the waiting. Six months, to be exact.

In the meantime, Lisa's tests had finally returned. I got the call and immediately shifted into action. We were to go and collect the results, and that there was no need to bring Lisa. Mam came, as she always did. The doctor sat me down. She wanted me to hear the results from her and not anyone else. I was informed that Lisa's mitochondrial disease would affect her muscles and other parts of her body. She had also found a Complex 4 respiratory chain deficiency strain which causes problems with the skeletal muscles, heart, kidney, liver brain, and with sucking and swallowing.[1]

Now that we knew the strain, we were asked to come in at a later stage to see the medical team when all results were returned. Nothing else was said — only that Gerry and I shouldn't blame ourselves. It just happened that two people came together that were not genetically compatible. It's very rare, we were told, but it can happen — and it had happened to us.

The news had coloured much of the months that came after, until the time came for my own results. In my heart, I knew. I sat there, waiting; every part of me felt numb. I was called in and sat before my fate.

I, too, had mitochondrial disease.

They told me that I had a Complex 4 strain, and, as if that wasn't enough, I also had a mild case of MS. "Do you have any questions?" The neurologist asked.

I remember looking at her. I could barely think. I looked at her and said, 'No.' Nothing that she could possibly say had the power to make me feel any better.

---

[1] GARD-> Genetic and Rare and Diseases information Centre.

Nobody could take this back. My heart was broken in so many ways —

for me, for my children, and for my husband, Gerry.

CHAPTER FIFTEEN
GRANT ME THE POWER TO ACCEPT

—◆•◆—

I t's a universal truth that mothers and parents forget themselves in those moments when their children need them the most. For us, this becomes problematic because beyond having seven kids with completely differing needs, three of them require our attention literally all of the time. The result is that we forget ourselves far more often than we remember. In all the planning and preparation, the work and the stress and the constant care, we forget that we have needs too. We are human, and we need taking care of. For parents who have children with autism, or a serious illness like mitochondrial disease, mental health is a point that needs to be stressed in large letters. We need to be reminded of it, and often. It matters a great deal because you just can't deal with others' problems when your own mind is in a bad place. Being a parent to autistic or severely ill children means you need to work with a clear head at all times. You can't afford not to. When you first sit on a plane, they teach you that if a plane begins to plummet, you need to fight your reflexes and put on your own oxygen mask on first. This ensures that the most clear-headed and experienced person is now in a better position to help those who are less likely to succeed. In other words, when that plane is going down, your priority always starts with you.

The beginning was hard. When all of this started happening — with our children getting sick, the autism diagnoses, the hospital visits, the endless cycle of not knowing, I felt as if I was losing my mind. I felt lost and depressed, as though there was no light at the end of the tunnel. The task just seemed impossible, and far beyond anything I was capable of fixing. I felt as if I had failed my children in some way and this was almost unbearable. A thought eventually found its way into my head that life was over as we knew it and that I just didn't know where or how to start all over again, or if anything could ever really be good again. All of the good spiralled into something dark and terrible and toxic, and it robbed me of all sense. It's so easy to get stuck in a mindset of negativity, caught between thoughts:

What if anything ever happens to me? What will become of my children? Who would take care of them? What if somebody treats them badly? What if children in school are mean to them? What if? What if? What if?

Only now, that very thing had come to pass. I now had to contend with my own sickness. More than that, I couldn't imagine a world where I could let it win. I remember waking on one of the worst mornings of all feeling as though the whole world had closed in around me overnight. I felt as if getting up was a step beyond what I was now capable of. And then it became a habit; not wanting to get out of bed some mornings because of this mindset of fear. On those mornings, my husband did it all: He took care of the children, got them ready for school, prepared their lunches and organized their day simply because my thoughts and feelings had paralyzed me. I took a backseat and stopped living in the real world, and that's how I coped — by living in a world where coping became a matter of ignoring my own needs. Of course, this catches up in the end. Looking back, I can see now how much of that time was panic and fear. It was all a great waste of time and energy; time I should have used to quietly organize things into boxes, to quieten my mind and start tackling one problem at a time; time I should have used to fix myself first before I even began tackling my other boxes — but that was then. I've learned from this time that, as much as we might want to fight the idea, life really is what you make it. Eventually, 1 put myself back together, lay my cards straight across the table and decided that I was going to make the most of what I had.

Time was my enemy at the beginning of it all, the constant organizing, the work it took to plan out a day, to deal with a meltdown, to do something that would only take a tenth of the time for a normal parent, all of it made me feel as though I had no time. Despite all this, I had to find time for me in order to survive — to succeed and to thrive for my kids. And if you can't find time, you have to make it. Start by making changes in your child's routines; small ones that create little pockets of time. 1 started making plans to move forward, speaking to as many people as 1 could about autism and mitochondrial disease to try and understand what I was dealing with. I wanted to understand what progress was being made and how I could use that progress to make things work for us. I had to make peace with the present, knowing that none of it would be easy, and that I could not change the children's condition, but I could change the way we dealt with it, and I could change my own mindset both towards the task and towards myself and what I deserved. The changes that we made to give them more freedom, more independence, meant that we had less planning to do, less things to remember, less meltdowns to deal with, and with all of this came more time. None of this would have been possible without a clear mind.

The will and the creativity would never have appeared if I had not started to talk to others, to recognize the issues I was facing as a result of my neglect. I had been eating from their plates in both a literal sense, gaining weight from the stress as I forgot about clean eating and my own health, and in a not-so-literal sense by absorbing their chaos rather than effectively dealing with it. Change starts with accepting that which can't be changed, and seeing with a clear mind what's possible and what's in your control.

CHAPTER SIXTEEN
NOT BEING DEFINED
BY AN ILLNESS

———•◦•———

T he hospital call finally came in the summer of
'09. We were called to a meeting where all our
results would finally change hands. Everything
they knew about our strains of mitochondrial
disease, all the starting points we needed to start moving
forward, to start navigating our life from here on with this
disease now sat in the hands of our doctor. It felt like a
bomb ticking under our feet; one that you couldn't
predict. One that could go off at any given moment. There
was no cure for any of this. It's all just a waiting game.

What they didn't say, if they even knew then, was that this invisible disease could take any of the children away from us at any time — at a moment of its choosing. It works its way into your body, setting its hands on every part of your insides, and you live knowing that it's there, knowing that nothing can be done to slow it down or get in its way. It's there in every moment, present at every event, awake even when you sleep, and it doesn't take vacations. You can't see it, but it's always present, always working. This was now our truth.

We travelled together to the hospital — to Dublin — for our meeting. We parked the car and sat for a moment. When we got to the hospital gates, Lisa started to scream and she cried all the way in. This was a place that she knew. She remembered the blood tests, the smells and the colours, the doctors and their questions, and that every other test one could think of had been done to her in this place. We sat in the waiting room — soothing her as we waited to be called. After a time, we were all called in and sat down like always. The children were brought over to the toys and they sat, like children. She started with an apology and that she would help us in any way that she could. She then told us that Sean had complex 4 mitochondria. Lisa had complex 4, which we knew at that stage, but it was Darragh's results that stood out the most.

"He has two strains: Complex 2 and 4," they said. I looked at her and asked how it was possible that Darragh could have two strains. I looked at my boy, believing that I knew Darragh's autism — that it was not as bad as the others. It didn't make sense.

It had been clear for a while that Sean and Lisa's conditions were progressively getting worse. I could see it. But Darragh was different. Or so I believed. As it turned out, Darragh's mitochondrial strain was worse than any of ours. His strain could turn into Leigh's Disease. And if that happened, he would be left with only a few years to live.

I inevitably asked the only question left to me: what was going to be done? We were told that all the tests that were available in Ireland at the time had already been done. There were, however, new tests that were being brought into the country, and we were on the waiting list. I heard the words, and still, I could only feel the concrete in my lungs, and the invisible hand around my throat. I felt as if my world was crushing down on top of me; as if something had dedicated itself to my misery. At the same time, there was another, smaller voice; something in the back of my mind that kept telling me to fight, and that it would only be over if I let it be.

They gave the children something called Q10 which was supposed to give them energy, and that was all we had to fight with. From there, the regularly scheduled appointments continued to keep track of changes, and to see if anything had progressed. It was stressed that if any of our children became sick, we would have to go directly to the hospital and without delay. The consequences, we were told, were great.

We left the hospital in silence and brought the children to McDonalds. It's what they wanted, and we could barely deny them. And in silence, we drove back to Galway. I remember being told that this was just a waiting game — that it might only be a matter of time before things take a turn. They couldn't tell us how long our children would live, only that each year should be cherished.

This is something no mother or father should ever have to hear.

I decided there and then that I was going to find out everything I could about this disease that was affecting my children, this disease that could change everything in a blink of an eye, and without warning. I would educate myself on every complex associated with mitochondrial disease and their effects. I needed to be prepared. I began researching everything. I read everything I could get my hands on; books, articles, you name it. I began to plan for all the things that might come, all the decisions that we might have to face. There were big changes on the horizon, and I believe that you can choose to live your life in two ways in response: you can either let your illness define who you are and live your life according to its every whim, or you can live your life the way it ought to be lived; every moment ought to be lived with happiness, with love in your heart, making every minute count, and making as many memories as possible with the people you love. It became my resolve to keep life positive. I believed that this illness was just an illness, it is not who we are in the here and now.

CHAPTER SEVENTEEN
NO WOMAN IS AN ISLAND

———•·•———

W

e began to live more consciously. Every day needed a positive effort and good perspective. It was this same mentality that allowed us to settle. We had to move forward. At the same time, our finances had taken a beating. We were finding it hard to make ends meet; renting the house, managing the bills and an endless line of hospital appointments. Moreover, though we had moved from one place to another, this house was also a temporary location until we found a place here that we could afford — a place to call home. We realised at this time that we needed help, and we needed a home. Knowing what we now know, we realised that we could no longer keep moving. It was at this time that we met Ciaran Cannon T.D. A gentleman, and a source of great change in our lives. Our cause found its way into his hands, and he promised to help us, and that he did.

It was evident, he said, that things hadn't gone well for us in the past, but this was about to change. We gave him the paperwork for all of our children, and in return, he gave us his personal mobile number and said to call him anytime. He came to our house, and often, he would look at our notice boards; we had two of them on the wall with all our appointments, and we were told that he would do all that he could to make it easier for us. He fought for us and came up against a number of walls on many different occasions but he never gave up. He kept going till he got us what we needed. And in hindsight, I truly wonder how we would have coped, and where we would now be without that help.

After two long years, things fell into place with Ciaran's help. We arrived at a house that you could only wish for; a six bedroom house with its own land. The bedrooms we needed were downstairs where the children would be safer. It had wheelchair access and room for our children to be outside; to be children, and to be safe. We moved in on Christmas Eve. It meant everything to us and our children, and it was thanks to Ciaran who believed in us, and in our cause. This is how things slowly began to change, and how we began to feel as if life could feel positive once more.

Ciaran, I believe, was meant to be brought into our lives. He helped us in ways we could never have imagined with all of the most crucial parts of our lives; with our children's needs, with the house and he also opened the unit in Sean's school. Moreover, when new problems came, he helped us to find solutions. When the children were diagnosed, we were informed that you are only permitted to be a carer for two sick children; having three, we had no choice but to get a carers allowance for Lisa in order to cover her care and needs. Furthermore, it was decided that Gerry had to be her carer. If Gerry went back to work, we would have lost more than we could ever regain. They would have taken our medical cards, and we would never have been able to pay the endless hospital bills. Our children's medication alone was the equivalent of four mortgages for a first-time buyer in the current climate. It was simply not possible. Nonetheless,

Gerry being at home all the time was great for our children, and frankly, for me.

Throughout all of this, though I worked hard to make peace with all of these things that forever threatened to do away with my peace, every day became a battle, and I found myself waking almost as tired as when I went to sleep. It was Gerry who encouraged me to retrace my steps to a spiritual path, to find a way to channel this difficulty, and to look for groups that could help guide me through everything that I felt.

It was my wish for my parents and siblings to see it all. We wanted to share this so much with my mother who had always supported us in every way.

She would have loved it.

Sadly, it was not to be, as my mother had a stroke during this time. I can't describe to you in words what I suffered at this point in life; only that with every good thing, I almost came to expect that it would forever be evened out by the universe — that every good came with a price. I sat for days, picking up the pieces of my own state of mind, just to be a mother to my children, and a wife to my husband. They told us that she had suffered a stroke in both sides of the brain, and, as it would come to pass, she entered a coma for what became three long months of our lives. Despite both hemispheres of the brain suffering, and without one to compensate, she somehow survived; something that none of her doctors could understand. With time, she gradually woke up and regained her mind in parts. The next greatest milestone came on the day she walked with the help of a frame; this was deemed to be a miracle. It simply shouldn't have been possible given what she had suffered. In the months that followed, we took her down to Galway whenever we could. This was her wish, and she strongly made her wish clear. For months, our mother who had been with me during every step, who had supported me and all our decisions, who had been there for everything, insisted on being with us in Galway. Even in illness, she persisted. Then, some months later, she eventually took one last deep breath, and that was to be her last.

I say all of this to make a single point: people, no matter what stage of life you're in, or regardless of what you're facing, life can be an incredible force — and source — of good. Without people, our thoughts end up bouncing around, never being questioned in our own mind. We end up believing the things we tell ourselves; the things that grow out of stress and struggle.

We let go of the idea that we have to do this alone, and the moment we reach out to others, things improve. This isn't always the case, but it's certainly true that none of us are made to be invincible. And none of us are meant to be alone in our struggle. I believe that pride can kill a person as easily as stress; believing that you can't possibly let people know that you're suffering, or that looking for help, or reaching out, is a sign of weakness, or giving up. Ciaran was, for us, so much of that difference. It was the ground we needed beneath our feet when our toes couldn't feel the bottom. Each day was just a matter of treading water, trying to stay afloat, and it was thanks to him that we could find the room to breathe.

For us, my mother was also a source of unlimited support in our lives. She gave us so much even when she had to fight in order to give it. She attended our appointments, she was always a call away when we needed her, and she was always present in any way she could be. Until the end, she was extraordinary.

CHAPTER EIGHTEEN
AND THEN CAME JAMIE

—◆·◆—

There was a time of grieving, and a time of recovering — as life tends to carry on whether you're paying attention or not. It came time to move forward, and there were new challenges to be met. I've spoken about change as something that each of us struggles with, but it's also the reason why sadness can eventually turn into joy. Everything changes with time, as we were about to be reminded.

Six years before, we made an application for an assistant dog for Lisa. We didn't really know at the time whether getting an autism-assistant dog would do anything for Lisa; whether it would change her life in any way. Despite her severe autism and being non-verbal, Lisa was still quite happy to be in her own world. As she grew, she began to enjoy being taken out on walks, and even shopping trips. But as she grew older it became a struggle. We found ourselves on constant alert as Lisa began to run off without any sense of danger. It took all of our focus to keep her safe. In the beginning, Lisa did not respond to her name being called, she would just stand there flapping as she looked into her own world and it all came to a point when her safety was no longer as manageable.

Six years on from our application, on December 2018, a notice came telling us that Lisa was to be given an assistant dog. Our response was excitement, wonder, and relief. Gerry and I were told to travel to Cork for three days where we would be trained for an assistant dog; and we were told that his name was Jamie. Truth be told, we were both skeptical and unsure as to how useful this would all be, until we met. We could barely believe how much intelligence and awareness Jamie possessed. He took to us straight away and we loved him from that first moment.

On the third day, we packed up and brought Jamie home to our very excited children. In the days that followed, we could see subtle changes in Lisa's behaviour and demeanour. She easily acknowledged Jamie's presence; something she had never done before. We have another dog, our Yorkshire terrier, Kim. Lisa had always been more passive around her; she wouldn't rub her head due to her sensory issues. And yet now with Jamie, she started to let him sit beside her and would even touch his coat.

The first time that Jamie really surprised us is when we first witnessed him during one of Lisa's meltdowns. Her meltdowns are very loud and full of movement; not the sort of thing that dogs tend to be attracted to. In that moment, Jamie walked straight over to Lisa, not one bit phased by what was going on, and lay down beside her making his presence known. Soon afterwards, she start to wind down. Each of us looked at each other, and then to Jamie, and to Lisa; none of us could believe it.

Since Jamie came into Lisa's life, she has become open to touching other animals, and even feeding them. She now loves to be in their presence — something that makes it easier to bring her to new and different places where there are lots of animals. Because of Jamie, she no longer carries any fear towards them, and this has brought so much joy into Lisa's life. One of our greatest reasons to love Jamie, however, is bedtime. As all parents of autistic children know, their children have a very difficult relationship with sleep. For as long as Lisa has been in a bed, she has always gotten up at least half a dozen times, which meant that we would have to keep putting her back in. She tends to wake up in the middle of the night and stay awake for hours. By morning, everyone found themselves exhausted; everyone except Lisa. Jamie changed all of this. Now, when bedtime comes around, Jamie finds his way into the bedroom, and he lies on his bed beside her, and stranger still, she loves him being there. She doesn't get out of bed anymore, and if she wakes in the middle of the night she doesn't get out of bed as she sees Jamie beside her. Only on one occasion did she leave the room, and Jamie went with her. He followed her into our room, came over to my side of the bed, and woke me up. He made me aware that both he and Lisa were there.

Jamie knows that Lisa is special. He knew from the first day he met her and still knows to this day. He knows her routines, he knows when she goes to bed, he even leads the way for her into the bedroom. They are a double-act; and they are both extraordinary together. More than that, Jamie has helped all of us. It's because of him that we now sleep more often, and for longer. He has also helped Lisa, and even the other children, with their sensory difficulties in meaningful ways. When we wash Jamie or brush his coat, Lisa gets involved, and so do Sean and Darragh. He has helped our kids to move past many of their limitations that existed because of their autism. He has enabled Lisa to have a social life as we can now bring her out to restaurants, to shops and on walks to the beach. Jamie walks with her, and she is attached to him and he takes care of her. He always minds her and stands in front of her when she tries to walk away. Jamie has brought so much freedom to our whole family; freedom that allows us to do so much more that we couldn't have done before. As well as watching Lisa, he also watches Sean and somehow understands that the same dangers exist with him. Beyond being helpful, he has brought joy and fun and laughter into our home as all our children want to play with him and he is always happy to oblige with great enthusiasm. It is because of his love and affection, his consistent care and attention that he has become a part of our family, and a best friend to a non-verbal autistic girl who once lived in her own world; a girl who can, for the first time, now socialize with a best friend of her own. He has made life for all easier and more peaceful than we can ever express in words alone. We love him dearly and we will forever be grateful to Autism Assistance Dogs Ireland for bringing Jamie into our lives. For us, Jamie represents change, and how letting change into your life can truly change it for the better.

CHAPTER NINETEEN
FUTURE GOALS

—·—

The future is never certain, and least of all for us. And still, when we're asked what our goals are, I always respond with *milestones*. Everything that we do is aimed at giving our children a life — a future beyond us, or at least one with a greater quality of life and some amount of freedom. That's the goal. If you ask me what to expect of them in ten years' time, I can't really say that I have an answer, but I can tell you what I hope for. It's our aim for Darragh to go to college. Even with his autism, I really think it's within him; he has the capability, the awareness, the potential. His greatest stumbling block is currently his anxiety. He's anxious about the places he goes, of being alone, of something going wrong, or being misunderstood and having no one to guide him. Even now, our closest goal is for him to enter secondary school where he will be faced with many new people, and just as difficult — many rooms. This will be his test.

For Darragh, not panicking when it comes to finding his way around will be a great struggle that he will have to overcome. If he can't find a room, he won't ask anyone for help. It just won't happen. Our hope is to give him the confidence, and that the people he meets in secondary school will give him a chance, and that they will support him and, in turn, give him confidence in who he is. The trouble is that the world is not kind, and people — let alone children — can be difficult around things they don't understand. We are scared, but we're hopeful.

So, too, are we scared for Sean's future. The question that we keep asking ourselves is: Where does he go after junior school? The truth is that there's so little in this country for kids with autism. His journey to some form of independence will be so much harder than Darragh's, and it's our belief that secondary school will not be a likely option. It's difficult for us to see Sean ever gaining complete independence due to the severity of his autism, and as a result, he will likely need to attend a school that better suits his needs. With Sean, our goal is more vague. It's a matter of exploring just how much independence he's capable of achieving, and then deciding on a path along the way as he gets older. There are no concrete solutions for him, and it's up to us to discover for ourselves.

The difficulty with Sean is that he lives in a world where it's a kid's cartoon. It's not real. Everybody's nice. It's a world where he can trust everybody and everyone's going to do the right thing for him. Our challenge is to teach him about the world around him, to help him understand the nature of things and what to really expect beyond his front door. For Sean, this is not a concept that's likely to come easy. It will take all of our effort, our creativity and our will to slowly expose him to a greater level of truth, and finding a way for it to make sense to him so that he might understand. Like Lisa, he does not fully understand the concept of danger. As children, we learn this by falling, by being exposed to pain and accidents. From those experiences we learn important lessons and we remember them as we move forward, but for Sean this is not the case. Not in the way that we know.

And so how do you give a child with autism this same experience in a way that doesn't put them in danger?

Lisa is a whole other matter. It's true that she has made great progress thanks to Jamie. He has opened up her world to animals, to the outdoors, to going for walks and being exposed to a wider world without fear. Nonetheless, Lisa will never live away from me. This, I understand. As a non-verbal child, she relies on my understanding of her needs through non-verbal means. This is not something that compliments independent life. Nonetheless, there is so much potential in Lisa, and like all children with autism, she has a talent, and talents can be grown. We believe in her talent, but also in her ability as a person.

It's my belief that Lisa might one day have words. We want to teach her to communicate more effectively, to tell us when she has a pain in her stomach, or that she's hungry, or scared — even if only via sign. At this moment, we're her tool, and through us, she gets what she needs. If we can teach Lisa to better communicate her needs to others, however, then her world becomes so much easier. She knows what she wants. She now picks and chooses. She makes decisions, and this is a great leap from where we first started.

We've come to understand that you need to put things into effect years before in order to see results. You need to plan so much further ahead for your children. As it is with all parents, we not only wish to do everything we can now to better their futures, but to nurture their gifts while they're still young, and even this takes planning. It's been seen that children with autism can express themselves through their talents in ways that reach through their condition and bring out everything that lies beneath it. It's our hope to nurture Lisa's love of music and to help her to find joy in it, to express herself through it in whatever way she can. We know that Sean loves to draw and to paint, and we hope to see a time when Sean can use painting as a way to express himself, to release whatever he's feeling through his art and to find happiness and peace through it. We believe that Darragh's potential will also accomplish great things for him. His understanding of computers and code is incredible, and if nurtured, it has the potential to give him a great deal of independence and fulfilment. And it's our aim to enable them. Of course, there is also the matter of time and all the things that come with it. We are against residential care should it ever come to that. These children are remarkable, and we believe that they deserve a place that is familiar; a home where they can continue to grow in a place that makes them feel safe. And though nothing about the future is certain, if we know anything, it's that we always find a way.

CHAPTER TWENTY
THE LITTLE THINGS MATTER

~.~

As we sit here and write this, we are surrounded by the typical chaos that is an ordinary day in our home. Sean is in the sitting room with a TV and an iPad in front of him, each streaming YouTube videos of Spongebob Squarepants; his favourite show that is always on in our house. Each of us can quote any episode at this point, much to our amusement. The sitting room opens into the sunroom where Lisa is sitting in front of a different TV with other cartoons on. In the corner of the room is where Darragh sits at his computer with his headphones on. The noise coming from each TV or tablet is already loud enough but Lisa has decided that she's going to walk around knocking down whatever she pleases, making that 'aghhhh' noise that she always makes to communicate her emotions. At the same time, Sean is shouting for his Daddy to bring him juice, and elsewhere throughout the house, the usual arguments between my eldest children shoot back and forth. I overhear something about the internet being slow because of all the videos that Sean and Darragh are streaming at the same time. But these are good problems. This is as close to normal as life can now ever be.

When people come into our home, they see absolute chaos where we see a typical, uneventful day. And yet, behind this picture is the difficult-to-see reality that it has taken so much in order to achieve even this.

Our family has come through endless ordeals, and though it might not seem like progress from the outside; to us, this is a world away from where we began. We have learned to make peace with what we can't change, to ask for help when we need it, to close our eyes and breathe when things become difficult. There is now a structure to our lives that we have built with our own hands, and with the help of people like Ciaran who continues to support us.

Our friends often struggle to understand how we relax when the house is this mad. The truth is that after years of repetition, all of this has become routine. Simply put: we've become used to it. Gerry has his own routine of making the dinners and getting the kids ready for bed. We've learned that because Darragh, Sean and Lisa have different levels of autism, that they each need their own routine; and their routines are anything but the same. It's like organised chaos, but we make it work. This is how we live our lives, and though it can be hard at times, it's also rewarding when one of our children reaches another milestone; milestones that were first thought to be impossible to achieve because of their conditions. It's for these milestones that we work, to allow our children more independence and a greater quality of living. This is what gives us our joy — our peace. We continue to live each day as it comes knowing that day is precious to us. In terms of our state of mind, it's hard to say that any of us are completely healed in every way. There is always a new obstacle, and so much to make peace with. But I know that I am a healing process in progress. I feel that I am at the beginning of my spiritual journey, and I've found that I am learning every single day, not only from spiritual teachers, but from my children too.

One of my greatest motivators for sitting down and writing this book was to help anyone with sick children or children with autism; for them to see that they are not alone, that they and their children have a voice, that no one ought to be alone in this struggle, that you have to fight for what you need, and that there is a way forward. I want to tell you that life can be lived in a positive way and that things can get better. If this book ends up in the hands of one person, and if only one person is helped at the end of it all, then I would be happy knowing that I helped at all.

Gerry and I want to tell each person that reads this that we do what we do with the help of everyone around us, and not just by ourselves. It will never be easy, but that doesn't mean that it can't be done. Now, as I write this, I don't feel as though Gerry and I are trapped. We love each of our children, and each of them bring us a great deal of joy. Together, we find joy in the little things. We enjoy the silence that we find in every day, we enjoy the days when the children can be children, when they play and laugh and sing. We look forward to family days out now that we know that those, too, are possible. And in all of these small things, we find a great deal to be grateful for; it gives us peace.

GUEST CHAPTER
(GERRY)

T he transition from what you perceive, or what you have perceived to be the normal life of a carer, to actually being one is difficult. There is help in place for your children, of course. There's medical support and different therapies they attend, and so on. But what is not nearly well enough understood are the problems that parents or carers go through in coping with this transition from normal to caring for autistic children. We tried to keep as much of our old lifestyle as we could. But it soon became clear that it wasn't going to work. The responsibility of caring for children with special needs is all consuming; we had entered into a new world of which we were very unsure; one that we had to give all of our attention; all of our energy;

All of our time.

Because of our uncertainty, we were always looking to others; to doctors and therapists for answers on how to live our lives. But what we got was not what we expected: You're the carer. It's all about the children now and you just have to accept your place. Not the easiest of things to hear. A lot of carers are starting to arrive at that realisation, believing it to be true; believing that this is a sentence, a terrible thing that has now been put on your shoulders. But what we can tell you is that this is not the case at all; not from our experience, at least. It's not our aim to tell you that it's not difficult, because it very much is; our aim is to tell you that it can co-exist with happiness and positivity, and even joy.

For most carers, your day looks something like this: you put your children to bed, praying that they sleep, because god knows what time they're going to wake during the night, and you never know how exhausted you're going to be in the morning. Children with autism have a tendency to not need as much sleep as most people. If they wake up, they're up all night. We can really testify to this, as we needed a special medicine to help them to sleep normally — or as close to it as possible. The repetitive nature of their lives can be mind-numbing to carers; every day is a copy of the day before. They eat the same food, and at the same time; they watch the same programmes over and over and over — happy in their repetitive existence. Nobody comes to your house anymore because it upsets the routine. These children just do not like change. You become uncomfortable with people coming to the house because you've been living this life for so long, completely immersed in your children's lives and their routines. You have practically isolated yourself from society. This is not your fault.

As we stated in the beginning, you have to give your complete attention to these children. And trying to carry on what society deems to be a normal life would likely break you. You cannot have the same life and be a carer; they are too different from one other. Instead, you have to learn to accept, and with what you now have, to move forward and find new ways to integrate it with a life of fulfillment. Ignoring reality does not help. The longer it takes you to realise this, the harder it becomes. You are not autistic, yet you are at all times surrounded by it and it becomes a huge part of your day. Some families cannot cope; they split, they can't accept the change, they can't cope with losing their old lifestyle, and they come to only see a future full of fear and non-existence. This is not a dramatic case, and though it is certainly not the truth; the belief that it is the truth is very real for many carers until they learn to accept the change, to move forward instead of fighting to hold on to the past. And it's true that sometimes, our reality can be a lot darker than what we've outlined here, but there is also so much more. Just as it is with life; there are always two sides. Our own journey was just like this.

Your first question is likely to be: How do we begin to cope? From one brace of carers to another, we work and collaborate to try and get a handle on this situation; on life. Beyond that, our mission is to tell you our story in regards to autism; the changes, the trials, the meltdowns, and the whole journey from there to here.

For those who care for children who have regular meltdowns, it can be overwhelming. More than that, it can be isolating. When you try to explain this phenomenon — and that's what it is — those who haven't witnessed a child having a meltdown in this way can't understand.

"You must be exaggerating? Surely nothing is that bad!" It's difficult to realize that a lot of people just don't get it. Let's take our daughter, Lisa. Lisa is severely autistic.

She is nine years old and non-verbal. Nearly all autistic children like Lisa are highly sensitive to a lot of things; sound, light, colour, touch, and even smell. This is fundamental to understanding what causes a meltdown. Sadly, no expert could ever have told us this. The only thing that has taught us is our own experience, our observations — and we'd like to pass this knowledge to you.

The first thing you need to know is that you have to observe everything when a meltdown starts. *Everything.*

Write it down, or keep a mental note. Sit beside them, go in to their world and ask: What's changed? What's different? Travel back a few seconds and compare the immediate past with what you now hear, who can you hear, what's on television, what you're sitting on, what you smell, how you feel. Sensory changes have a huge impact and are a very large trigger for these events. Observation and focus is always going to be important here — especially when it comes to situations you think are beyond your control. The truth, however, is that you do have much more control than you think. A great deal of it is practice, it's a muscle that you have to exercise to make it stronger and more capable. Think of yourself when you're stressed or anxious — what kind of energy are you exerting? What emotions are you expressing and how are you expressing them? If you're cooking on a bad day then you might end up making a lot more noise along the way. You might find yourself talking loudly on the phone when you're stressed or trying to solve problems. You might even be cooking with something new or different without realizing that doing this is significant.

These things can trigger your child's meltdown. Children with autism are very sensitive to everyone and everything around them — especially those closest to them. They feel your emotions, and this is a trigger for them.

It's difficult to identify yourself as the source of a problem. Of all the things that might come to a new parent's mind about what may have triggered their child's meltdown, the last thing they might ever expect is themselves. Your child's other senses are heightened far above your expectations. Trust us. They focus in a way that we rarely do. They have to, as this is the only way they can maintain a sense of calm. But what they sense the most is what they rely on most, and that's you. Now these other things; sound, light, touch, colour, and smell — they sense these things more than we do, and in turn, it affects them more. It has to be said that if it weren't for Áine helping me to understand her process, that is, what she was doing to control Lisa's meltdowns, I would probably be none the wiser today. It's easy to feel helpless and out of control but there are methods

My favourite story is the following, and it provides a good example, though Áine might have a few choice words about this. But I insist because if it helps other carers then it has to be told. I remember walking into the house one day to be greeted by a vision of my lovely wife flapping her arms in the air like she was trying to take off. Now my first thought was: the poor woman, she has finally lost it. I had better ring for somebody. Anybody! But as I walked into the room, smiling, it became clearer. There was Lisa standing in front of her, also flapping her arms, as is a common trait of autism. This might seem beyond logic, and a lot of the time, a great deal of what we do might seem that way, and this is why we choose to share our story.

Because none of this is written in a textbook. Our path to understanding and coping has entirely been made with the help of our own creativity and our willingness to try things that might seem crazy. As I stood there in the room, I realized that, for a few minutes, Lisa's world of isolation had been completely broken down. You could see by the smile on her face that she shared some sort of understanding with her mammy, and that they were sharing minds. You could see the connection between them, and this mattered far more than the method of getting there. At this point in my story, I should say that you shouldn't be afraid of meltdowns. The more you fear them, the less in control you'll be, and the more difficult it will be to deal with them.

Remove negative emotions, when faced with one; this won't help you, or them. Study, observe and use each event to understand what triggers them, and how to lessen the length and severity of each one. For us, it took a great deal of learning, of being afraid as parents not knowing how to correctly deal with them, or if there even was a "correct way." Today, Lisa's meltdowns are significantly shorter in time and lesser in their severity. This didn't happen by accident. Now, Lisa knows she is not alone, and there are ways in which Áine can go into her world with her, working with her emotions, easing her mind, which brings her back to us each time with a smile on her face.

RETURNING TO ÁINE

—◆•◆—

I have, of course, gotten to a stage where I wanted to give up, but I have come to the realisation, as a parent, that if we give up; all is lost. I believe that our children are given to us for a reason. Perhaps that reason is that we were the best suited to take care of them; or that they set us on a path that gave us the growth we needed to navigate life; maybe both. Not all blessings are obvious to us at first. Know that your child wouldn't be who they are today if it wasn't for you and the care you have given them. Even though you feel that every day is a fight, that you still fight for them is a mark of your own strength, your virtues and your ability to make this life beautiful for someone beyond yourself. And each milestone they meet is because of your love and your support. You, too, are extraordinary, and perhaps that's why you were chosen.

As you might now see, no one could ever fill your shoes. In their mind, you are their world. Whether you hear it in words, or through non-verbal expressions, know that your child appreciates you for everything you do. There is an awareness, and they love you more than anything in this world, even though they might not be able to show it.

Our children know a lot more than we give them credit for. Sometimes that meltdown happens because they're sad, and your child might be sad because they also feel your sadness. They can't find the words to make us feel better, or they can't express their emotions through speech, and so the only thing left to them is to get your attention. Recognise that your child is aware, embrace them, take the time to see their meltdowns as something other than just a meltdown. There's always more beneath the surface. We find it so easy to blame ourselves for our child and the suffering that they go through. We convince ourselves that there was a fault in our actions, and that this fault is ours alone, when in reality, autism is just a fact of life. Each of us are wired differently and given different sets of circumstance, and there is no way of knowing who will be given what.

Who among all of us are ever exactly the same? There is a different path that we can walk with our child, not one of false positivity, but one of realistic optimism. Not "Everything is fine", but "Everything can be made better with the right mindset." If we embrace realistic optimism, our own potential, and the potential of our children, the possibilities become endless.

Acceptance in itself, is a milestone. It will change the way you look at everything. And this is how you cope. When we see our lives as a hardship, that is what we get, and what we find in everything that we do. In reality, what you choose to see is what you are more likely to find. So I urge you to choose wisely, to make peace with all that can't be changed, and to change what you can.

PART IV
ENDINGS ARE NOT ALWAYS ENDINGS

—·●—

CHAPTER TWENTY-ONE
THE HOUSE OF ADAM

—◆—

I 'd like to say it all ended there. We found answers, maybe a happy place, a resolution to the madness that's this house. I'd tell you that peace continued, but those sort of endings are at the end of other people's stories — at least for now. Peace isn't easily kept in our house, see. It comes for a while, sits down and takes a good look around. It settles into a warm groove, takes its time like, and then, somehow, something changes. Something small, although it's not usually that. Usually, it's big things. Disastrous things. All sorts of things you couldn't imagine as being part of anyone's normal routine. Well, this time, it was just like that: a disaster.

Not all disasters are made equal, and the year of 2020 promised a special sort of trouble that began with a news story in mid-March. Until now, everything was about the same as it's always been. Darragh clacking on a keyboard in a room somewhere, Sean watching TV repeating lines for fun, learning something new. I can hear Lisa screaming in another room as I write. And during all this, there was Adam — the introvert who quietly went about his day while everything else continued in chaos about him. For most of us, seventeen is a memory — summer things, the knowledge that school will soon end and something else will come after. It's probably our first taste of real fear, like the world you know is coming to an end, or like something bigger is about to take off. Whatever better is, who knows at seventeen? Life is good, right? He'd go to school, come home, plug in and listen to music for hours, quietly wanting to get out and go to college. While he never complained, his world needed silence, and also noise. In this house, we possessed more of the latter than the former, but in all the wrong ways.

For months now, Adam had been dealing with more bouts of being sick than any of us could help but notice as strange. It's a mother's instinct, a sense that something isn't right, that something just changed but you can't put your finger on the button. Adam had been feeling ill for months, and to my constant worry, it just wasn't going away. When Adam woke up one morning, getting on with his usual routine, he found something that presented like a lump.

At first, it wasn't much until Christmas came and Adam began to speak up. Of course, all the parts of me that worked in the background — even when I was tired or not really here — came together and decided that Adam needed to see a doctor. There were blood tests and the tests said everything was normal. I spoke to those around me and we all agreed that everything was fine. It was like things *had* to be fine. The alternative was terrifying. Eventually, they told us that it was a swollen node, and that's what it was until February — just a thing that was nothing really. Nothing at all. Not until it became something.

The day that Gerry left with Adam was the day I stopped breathing for the several months that followed. It was as if it had left me and gone with them, and when they returned it was without whatever part of me that allowed me to feel air — to sit still and know some sort of peace. It was Adam, however, who couldn't breathe. His chest had been hurting, and it hurt all the way to the doctor where it subsided just as he arrived. On this occasion, Adam told us that the lump had gotten bigger. The doctors agreed and rushed Adam to hospital. They all got together out there, talking in quiet like doctors do, talking about Adam. All the talk did nothing but make Gerry nervous, of course. I wasn't there, but it all played out something like this:

"No way in Hell it's cancer," Adam had said. "It can't be."

Gerry shook his head, listing off all the reasons why it wouldn't be cancer. It couldn't. This was Adam — a seventeen-year-old boy. His life was school and music and goals of going to college. There was no room in all that for something like cancer. All the same, Adam went through tests and slept on a trolley in a crowded hospital not sleeping much and then sleeping until morning. The doctors, he said, surrounded his bed like bad news.

"Lymphoma," one of them said. A lot of people nodded.

When the doctors left, he sat in that hallway watching people just go by — 'normal' people. Nothing at all was connecting in a way we could understand.

"It just doesn't make any sense."

Any why would it? Adam was always in the background, always finding a way through the day — maybe that's what saved him? — In the end.

"Just don't whine about it and you'll be fine," Gerry said, joking, doing everything in his power to make room for laughter, to cut through the harsh reality. From the first moment Gerry knew, he was already present and fully prepared to take Adam's whole world on his shoulders. That was Gerry.

I remember coming home. Not much else, really. I cried like no one's business. I went into the bathroom and felt sick inside. Somehow, the floor became a pit, moving under me as I came apart by the bathroom sink, and I might have just given myself to it if it had only asked, but it didn't. And then, life went on. I asked all sorts of questions that night, like how you make your child feel alright with cancer? Where's the book that tells you how to make it all ok? And how do *I* cope with this? There were teams of doctors and specialists for the cancer, but the mental trauma was invisible; that's a thing that never makes it to the charts. They don't come to you and ask: "Well, how have you been coping?"

I might have said I wasn't coping. I might have said that I didn't even think this was real. I could have said things that would have painted a picture a little more like the truth, but that would have made it all harder. Knowing that the difficulties our youngest three faced had now arrived at Adam's door, only in a different form, should have broken him — and it nearly broke me. The choice to vanish into myself didn't exist. It couldn't. And still, how do you tell your son that cancer will work out? How do you show up to the job? And I wasn't alone in my struggle to believe. Gerry didn't believe it was true either. Shock does that to people. When he walked in that day — the day of Adam's diagnosis — Adam knew he'd been crying.

"Something got into my eye" Gerry said to him, of course.

He didn't know what to do, but he knew in his heart that he was going to get Adam through somehow. He just didn't have the words yet. For me, it felt like a dream you know you've had before: you know the kind that you wake up from just *knowing* that you recognize it somehow? Well, this was like that — a dream I've seen before. Only this was real life playing out like a broken record, playing the same tune and we all had to dance along to the music. It's a harsh way of painting your life, like it's something you're trying to get away from, but at the end of the day, a spade is still a spade.

For us, we're always learning new words to deal with grief, and the list grows year by year. Our vocabulary never stops growing, really. Our family learns new words all the time in ways few people do. There's a little book of medical terms — words and phrases that we all know. And in the aftermath of Adam's diagnosis — which we later found out to be stage II Hodgkin lymphoma — a new word entered our lives that sounded an awful lot like more grief. We didn't have time to worry about what went on in far off countries where, for weeks now, an epidemic was raging. Some people started to talk. Would it come here?

"Would what?"

"Coronavirus," they said. They told us about a virus, a thing that takes people with compromised immunities and —

"Lisa," I thought. "And Sean, and Darragh, and now Adam."

I don't know how I made it through those times. I still don't. For a while, no one believed COVID-19 would arrive at our door but just like cancer, it came when we least expected it, and it overturned everything in its path. Adam saw very little of this thing that started small and slowly turned into a nightmare. He'd come home on the day of his diagnosis, looked in the mirror and decided that this was just another thing to get through.

That was Adam's way. And so while Adam was adjusting to something that few of us will thankfully ever understand, we began to see our world change both inside and out as the numbers of people suffering beyond the front door began to climb, and the worry slowly escalated, and people began to panic. It felt like shouting at both ends. For me, I had clung to the 2% chance that the doctors had given us that Adam's lump was something else. I held on to it like one of those things they throw you at sea when you're

drowning. It had to be something else, for Adam —
for my boy — and for me. For all of us.

His first proper view of the outside world came
with treatment the following Friday. Things were
changing outside, and Adam, not wanting to face his
own trauma, came home and shaved his head in
expectation of what was coming. He didn't want the
grief of it — of waking up and watching his hair fall
out in clumps when he woke up in a world that was
falling apart outside.

The first two-and-a-half months took on a lot of
that feeling, like things you always took for granted
were suddenly falling apart. Like Adam getting
through his young years intact, or there being shops
with full shelves, or streets of people. When the
chemo started, Adam began to feel its effects,
comparing it to the feeling of life leaving you; when
it starts doing what it's supposed to do, it starts
hacking everything inside. It was, in his words, the
living embodiment of Hell trying to exist inside his
own body. There was a point when it drove him to
crisis. Gerry found him short of breath experiencing a
panic attack. He explained that it would go away, and
that everything was fine, but it never did stop. That

feeling of panic, of heart palpitations and barely being able to breath went on for Adam for as long as it took him to heal.

And throughout all this, all the other parts of our lives continued. Gerry and I were doing our best for the kids, trying to make Lisa's day as normal as possible, carrying out our routines — and, of course, checking in with our other three children who were living their own lives and yet still present in ours, always helping us find a way to cope. In the nights before, Adam had found the edges of his own sanity in a conversation with his father.

"I don't really care anymore. If something happens to me, that's it. I just don't care"

For all Gerry could see, his son had lost hope. His father told him how important it was to just keep going — for you. And if not for you, then for the people around you. That there was always something to live for. None of us knew then how important these words would become. For days, and then weeks, and then months it kept ringing through Adam's head — those words. I wouldn't hear them until much later when I needed those words as much as he did. I don't know if Gerry ever saw the difference — how much it changed Adam to hear those words. Adam started to come home, to fight through this thing as best as he could. And all that time, he did it for us, and he did it for Gerry. The lengths to which his father was willing to go to get him through can't be explained in words. Somehow, he always found the will and the strength to be there for his son, and for me. But life has a way of catching up, of undermining our peace just when we're ahead. In the living room, we sat together — Gerry and I — not so much pretending that all of it wasn't real as just trying out normal, I suppose. We watched a movie, something stupid that Gerry wanted to watch, I remember. We sat together like that, just the two of us. I'd been thinking of telling him about a dream — one that really had been recurring. In this dream, Gerry always told me he was leaving. And somehow, in that dream, Gerry always had a reason to go even though I'd beg him to stay. Yet somehow, he'd always vanish in the end. Here one minute and gone the next. But I'd always wake up, and there he'd be, snoring in bed. There for me, for all of us, just like he always was.

"You know," he said, turning. "You know when we go, we never really *go* — we're always around, somehow."

Those were his words — his last, as it would turn out in the end. He complained of pains in his neck, that something wasn't right. He'd gone for just a while to rest, it barely seemed like minutes. It took all of those minutes for a lifetime to end. On a quiet Wednesday evening just as our lives were settling, Gerry suffered a massive heart attack. And somehow, in this world of horrors, there was still space for one more:

Gerry was dead.

CHAPTER TWENTY-TWO
LOVE OF MY LIFE

erry, the father of my children, the foundation that had kept this house standing, lay in Adam's room. His eyes were turned toward the ceiling when our son found him struggling to breathe. "He's breathing weird, mum," Adam said. He knew that something was terribly wrong.

Everything of that night is like a tape that keeps playing in my mind. It never stops. Sometimes I go out and let the world get in the way of it — boring stuff life shopping, or taking the kids to school just to turn off, to pretend like it wasn't real. I'd think of how we ran into that room, froth bubbling at the corners of his mouth, the glassy stare in his eyes that you recognize in people when life leaves them. Gerry, in his final moments, looked like someone else's husband dying in front of my eyes, and I just happened to be here, watching. That feeling lasted all of a second, all of forever, and then panic took over. I saw those same eyes I'd seen in my mother the night she passed, looking at me and looking through me all at once. Some part of me knew that an enormous part of my life had just checked out forever — that this was all we were going to get. The love of my life; It was done. It was over. And there was nothing I could do but stare.

Sometimes, when I'm caught in traffic, I think about the minutes we spent trying to revive him, clinging to a phone while someone told me how to keep Gerry alive — like a spiritual medium keeping me connected to what I couldn't see any more in front of me. She told me to keep pumping, to give him air. That night, it felt like we were doing our best — Adam and I — to bring him back, and now I think I was keeping myself alive in that moment just as much. We didn't stop until the medics were outside our door, and then in the room, and then I was standing, and then I wasn't. Everything happened in flashes. I remember Adam helping Gerry's body to the ground. I watched the medics and the machines working away. At the same time, I saw myself in that picture looking at everything going on — and I was somewhere else in that room, watching myself while I broke into pieces.

"We need you to see the machine," somebody said.

They wanted me to see him flatline, to see hope dead and beyond saving. They wanted me to know that there was nothing they could do to bring Gerry back. Walking out of that room, I saw a circle of medics and members of the Gardai. They were all looking at me. I remember going to the room, crying until there was nothing left in me. Nothing to give that wasn't grief. Those memories are always there in my mind. They never go away.

Gerry died on 17th June, 2020. They took his body to the crematorium where, two days later, he was gone. The funeral — held in the middle of a pandemic — was as grim as you might expect. The younger children had no one to care for them, and so they came with us and attended their father's funeral not knowing what they were watching. Lisa struggled, of course, and Sean was there too, along with Darragh and the others. There was nothing we could do but let them be there.

I thought about the night he died, how Adam had watched me on my hands and knees begging him not to go. I remember how Amy told me she loved me; I could see the fear in her for what might come. There by his coffin, all the terrible memories of that night played out like someone else's dream, and I was forced to attend.

But then I watched my children leave with friends of ours to sit in McDonalds some distance away while we cremated their father because there was no one to mind them at such a devastating time. Everything felt like one big joke played by the universe. Amy had seen something in me that caused her to worry endlessly, as though Gerry's death wasn't enough. Dean held it together, as did Ryan, as they all did for a while. I can't speak to their grief, but none of us came out the same. Gerry was there for all of us, always.

The strange thing about death is that time still passes, and all those days where you're sitting at the traffic lights, or outside the school gates staring into nothing like a robot, feeling nothing — all that time is still life happening around you. Most days still consisted of panic attacks, school runs, and not knowing how I was going to keep doing this day after day. There were moments of forgetting, and then I'd hear his voice — I was looking for it in crowds, replaying old messages. Even the things he'd left about the room were somehow a living part of Gerry. Moving them, to me, seemed like a small death and so everything stayed in its place, and I would sit and stare at a pair of slippers, or listen to an old message in the bedroom until eventually the thought of going forward seemed impossible. And so, somewhere in those weeks after, I found myself on the floor begging for a way out of this mess. I needed a sign. And without a sign, I was genuinely afraid.

And yet somehow, in that spot, Gerry found me; his memory and my grief met, and he was there — for just a moment — holding me as though he had never left, his hand resting on my hair. We said nothing in our moment of peace, and for just a while longer, life was beautiful again. And that was enough. Enough to stick around, I'd decided — there in that moment.

The moment of true healing was much less spiritual than it was a devastating reminder. Kids, as it happens, are awfully good at getting to the point. Though I'd committed to suffering on without my husband, it was a stretch to say I slept, or functioned well, even. And standing in the door of the utility room one morning, my son took all the sense in the world and put in there in front of me like a sign.

"Are you going to die, too?" Sean said, looking as though he expected me to vanish at any moment.

"What do you mean?"

"Well, you're not looking after yourself. Are you going to leave me too?"

It was the second sign in so many weeks, and it hit just hard enough that everything — *everything* — came back into focus. That was when I realized that things needed to change.

"Of course I'm not going to die," I said. Those were the words I said out loud. But I had to believe it, too. I had to mean it.

Going back to a place from when I was a child, I walked all the way through the mess and into a place I used to go when life became too much. Call it a safe space. That's where healing started, in making a place

I could sit in my brain, a place made up of all the things that brought me peace. From there, I started reaching out, even left the house without any reason. I went out and bought things, had a coffee, normal stuff. I walked a little further, I met friends, and then I let people in. Of all the things that happened during that time, the kindness of other people reminded me more than anything else that there was still a world outside the front door. That life could somehow still exist despite everything. That was the moment of great change — the moment I knew everything would be ok. With everything that had happened, I had barely realized how much Adam was suffering too. His last words to Gerry were:

"I don't really care anymore."

Gerry had wanted him to live more than anything, and in the wake of his father's death, somehow, he felt as though he owed it to his father to keep going — to come home and get it done. And yet he'd seen his father die, had tried to bring him back to life, and he then had to sleep in that room and think it over while battling his own demons — his cancer. And so, after months of sleeping four hours a night, trying to find a way to live without Gerry, the last day of treatment had come for Adam and everyone felt it. We drove through a city that didn't look anything like Galway. People were wearing masks and gloves. Streets were empty. Everything felt different.

The pandemic hit the west coast like a wave, and everything under it was left strange and empty. And so, we drove on to the hospital. I remember how Adam talked about things that day as though his body knew what was coming. Despite everything, he smiled that day through his last injection knowing that the second and third day would hurt, and that afterwards came freedom. I can't imagine how happy Gerry would have been to have seen it. I imagine how much he would have smiled, how glad he would have been to have seen his son come out fighting, and believing again. Underneath, Adam missed his father more than anything. He had long decided that he couldn't go back to that house, not while knowing everything that had happened there. There was too much grief between the walls for Adam, and so when he left that hospital, he left home, too. He just kept on going.

The end of it all wasn't quite what we imagined, but some version of it did come in the end. I was talking to people again, and I was now finding a part of my old self — the one that had existed while Gerry was still alive, only now I was learning to live without him. The children were completely unaware that their father wasn't coming back, and every time I looked at Lisa as she screamed for her father, I was reminded of how much Gerry loved her, and how much she loved him. But with time, Lisa cried a little less, and things improved day by day. I know deep inside that what Gerry gave her, what he gave all of them is still there, still alive in their memory and no one can ever take that away.

Finally, a day arrived when Adam received a call. The nurses called and told him that he had gone into remission. I remember the sense that something terrible had passed, that light had come from somewhere. Adam had once said that cancer felt like losing your identity and finding a new one that knows all sorts of things that make life look different afterwards — like how good it feels to just be outside, to not be in pain. Adam's new world was a world with eyebrows, and that, according to him, was all right. I suppose my life was like that, too. Finding a new identity. Adam, remembering Gerry's words about getting through, and how everything would finally, somehow, be alright found his own way forward. And I found mine. And the kids found theirs. And so our story doesn't end with grief. I've learned to have gratitude for a wonderful family, for the twenty years I still had with Gerry. I learned that I have to be present, to come back to this world after sadness and live. Because the truth of it is that none of us are promised anything. All we get is life. And life is what happens whether or not we're paying attention.

CHAPTER TWENTY-THREE
HOPE & ALL THE REST

———•———

I t's a topic we were often asked to respond to: the future. There are parents with children who struggle with challenges of a different kind, and they look to our story for answers. There was a much younger version of us — of Gerry and I — who would have never believed it possible that we would have been the ones to provide the answers to their questions. And yet, there's a truth to the notion that we rarely lose ourselves on those roads well-travelled. We were always capable of rising to the task, and no part of us was last in becoming who we had to be. It had taken all this time for us to realize that we were here, even though Gerry has taken his seat earlier than anyone could have imagined, and that I am now writing this because we found a way. I now believe that we also have a duty to share everything that we've found — for all the younger versions of us who are only now beginning to find themselves at the foot of their mountain. And so came the need to write this book.

I'll admit, before I go on, that I had a different picture of life. I wish I could deny this; to say that I was prepared for every outcome, and that time has fully healed me. The thing is, as I passed the days, waiting for Darragh to be born, I watched other children playing outside, doing all the things that children are supposed to. And when Darragh was born, I caught myself, and often, sitting somewhere lost in that same picture — watching children play, watching them as they fell, and as they stood back up again. All on their own. I feel guilty for saying it, for wishing that those were my children, that my version of motherhood could look like that. I wish that Gerry were still here and that our family could look back in years to come on a different picture. There would still be, in every day, a maternal worry, the worries of normal people, but certainly not this. I believed, too, that I would live much more of my life with the man I loved, and even that is now something I have to reckon with.

It's not just us either; it goes beyond parents. What no one sees behind the suffering that we as parents shoulder is the weight that bears down on our other children. I remember the first time my eldest, Dean, pointedly told me that he never intends on having children.

It didn't immediately explain itself. I'd never had any reason to believe that he'd had any feelings towards the matter.

"It's that fear," he told me, "of living in the situation I've been in all my life."

No one wants to add to that. No child grows up through this and, down the road, imagines being a parent in the way that others do. What other people imagine is a world completely removed from our world, and all the challenges they've faced are challenges that no parent ever wants to see their child face. The typical idea of a parent is no longer a view that Dean or any of my others can believe in for their own future. This was my first lesson in collateral damage. You don't see the scale of the damage until a long time after. And this, as it turns out, was a war with many casualties.

In the event of our passing, we had discussed the future — that difficult problem that, until recently, we couldn't even begin to imagine. Our children deserve to live, and they deserve whatever version of normality we could give them — even if it means the difference between being eased out of a traumatic episode by a loving, familiar face, in a loving and familiar environment, as opposed to a new, strange place filled with unknown faces; with a new language; with nurses diffusing the madness that we have long come to terms with. The eldest three have spoken of taking one each and sharing the weight of our burden. They, themselves, are more than they will ever give themselves credit for; and no one will thank them; and no one will ever know their struggle. They are extraordinary in their own right for their courage in facing a theatre of war and choosing to wade in with warmth in their faces and love in everything that they do. I know that Gerry would have been proud of them regardless of the outcome.

So yes, I imagined it all a little differently. And as you've come to know in some way, we are not afforded a great deal of room to hope. Our family is one faced with endless challenges, and yet we are a family who have come through much more. Now, without Gerry, it is even more difficult to look forward with optimism; our lives are mirrored in chaos and yet we try so hard to be a picture of hope — and not only because we must. It's our true belief that this is not the end.

Our children — all of them — are extraordinary. The challenges that Sean, Darragh, and Lisa face are not entirely unknown to them. I truly don't believe this. This, in our minds, paints a clearer picture of how strong the human mind can be — that even in the face of such calamity within the body, our children can smile, even laugh, and at the rarest of times, if only for a flicker of a moment, they can even be children. That Adam could go through Hell and come out laughing is a further testament to healing. In the face of my own loss, this gives me more hope than I can say.

I am a parent of children. Seven of them. And our love — Gerry's love — for them was and forever will be boundless. But I would add a cautionary note, and it's this: you'll find guilt in so many places, and you'll find ways to carry it with you. Your love and your hope does not absolve the grief. There is also a great deal of false positivity in the world, acting as though everything is alright, and a self-sabotaging effort of pretending like you could never change a thing. This won't serve you in the way that you think; there are some things that can be changed. Perspective, instead, is how we cope. You are allowed to say that you wish things had gone differently — scream it if you have to. Denying this won't make you a better person, and it won't bring you any kind of lasting good. The truth of it is that ours is a heavy-handed struggle, and in it, we carve out for ourselves a path of acceptance; one that offers light; one that offers growth and sleep-filled nights and happy moments with — and sometimes without — loved ones in spite of it all. We move forward with faith in our abilities as people to adapt and overcome.

We acknowledge that life is a double-sided coin always turning. Happiness, just as it is with sadness, isn't made to last. One eventually replaces the other, teaching us meaning and appreciation. And so we cherish the good days, and we learn on the bad ones. In this way, we know that whatever lies ahead will be a result of our best human effort — and that we will have done it together. Despite everything, my children are still here with me, and our memories of Gerry will never be forgotten. In that, we can find a kind of happiness that can be carried forward.

For those of you in this same struggle — concern yourself less with what you're supposed to be. There will be times when all of your resources will fail to give you answers, and so you must make your own. There are times when you have to fight tooth-and-nail and demand the extraordinary. Have courage. So, too, will there be times when the future is a terrifying thought that waits for you at the beginning of every new day. Know that there is a road through it — as I am still finding a road through my own grief. But above all else:

There is hope.

EPILOGUE

—•—

Our much beloved husband and father, Gerry, passed away while writing this book. He was my entire world and he did so much to make it a great world to live in. He cared so much about those around him and his entire life was dedicated to the kids and to us. In writing this book, Gerry really wanted us to give hope to parents of children with mitochondrial disease, with autism, and with cancer. Though he can't be here with us to see it in its final form, he would no doubt have been glad to know that he contributed to helping someone even after death. Before his passing, Gerry and I wrote briefly on our own methods in navigating severe illness and we hope that it brings insight and peace. It's my hope that these words give to you as Gerry gave to all of us — something to live by, and something to live for. And, of course, I hope that it gives you hope as Gerry gave to everyone around him in life.

- Gerry & Áine

FIND THE AUTHOR

Find Áine Crosse on FaceBook at Áine Crosse
- ◊ Twitter at @AineMcAuleyCros
- ◊ Instagram AineLisaMcAuleyCrosse
- ◊ Pinterest Aine Lisa Crosse

Áine can be booked to speak and present by contacting
her Agent, Susan McKenna, at
info@bookhubpublishing.com
091/846953